KNITS
FOR MEN

KNITS
FOR MEN

20 SWEATERS, VESTS, AND ACCESSORIES

MARGARET HUBERT

Creative Publishing
international

Creative Publishing
international

Copyright © 2008
Creative Publishing international, Inc.
400 First Avenue North
Suite 300
Minneapolis, MN 55401
1-800-328-3895
www.creativepub.com

ISBN-13: 978-1-58923-359-1
ISBN-10: 1-58923-359-X

10 9 8 7 6 5 4 3 2 1

Library of Congress Cataloging-in-Publication Data
Hubert, Margaret.
  Knits for men : 20 sweaters, vests, and accessories / by Margaret Hubert.
     p. cm.
  ISBN 1-58923-359-X
  1. Knitting. 2. Men's clothing. I. Title.
  TT820.H835 2008
  746.43'2041--dc22   2007045662
                                          CIP

Technical Editor: Rita Greenfeder
Copy Editor: Karen Levy
Proofreader: India R. Tresselt
Book Design: John Hall Design
Cover Design: Howard Grossman, 12e design
Page Layout: Megan Cooney
Illustrations: Mario Ferro

Printed in China

Contents ||||

|||| About the Projects

Over the years, I have designed countless patterns for magazines and written several books on both crochet and knitting. I recently mentioned to my editor that although I've knitted untold numbers of special items for the men in my family, I've yet to write a book dedicated strictly to men's knits. "What a coincidence," she said. "That's exactly what I'd like you to do next!" That's all it took to get the wheels turning.

I've done my research and spoken to a lot of men—family members, friends, and perfect strangers—to find out what men like and dislike in sweaters. As you can imagine, the answers were quite varied, from bright colors to muted colors, from very lightweight to heavier weight, and from plain stitching to patterns, but the comment that I heard most was that a sweater must be comfortable to wear and loose fitting. Men also like attention to details. They like the little touches that make a sweater special, such as an intricate design, a different collar, zipper closings, and pockets. They also like a slightly different take on a classic style.

Some men love crew necks, others love V-necks. I have included several different neckline choices, so you can select the one that suits best. For each project, I chose a yarn to complement the stitch and design of the garment, using a variety of colors, from rich tones to neutrals. I used some lightweight yarns for warmer weather, and some medium- and heavier weight yarns for cooler temperatures. I chose plush alpacas, wools, soy silk, cotton, and some blends. Along with the generic descriptions of the yarns, you'll also find the exact brands and colors I used. You may substitute yarns, providing you get the same gauge called for in the project. Please make a gauge swatch for all your projects, no matter how confident you are. All expert knitters know that skipping this step is pure folly.

I have included several cardigans, pullovers, and vests as well as accessories such as hats, scarves, and slipper socks. Some of the projects are very easy and require a minimum of shaping and finishing—even a beginner will find them easy. Others are a little more challenging and will give all knitters the opportunity to learn new stitches and tricks—experienced knitters will enjoy them, too.

The Tips and Tricks section provides some insight into getting the proper fit and finishing your knits like a pro. The Knitting Basics section serves as a general guide for the terms and techniques used throughout the book. With careful planning and attention to details, you'll knit garments that will be worn and enjoyed for years to come. I hope that you enjoy the book and are inspired to try a different take on knitting for men.

Margaret Hubert is also the author of *Hooked Bags, Hooked Hats, Hooked Throws, Hooked Scarves, Hooked for Toddlers, Plus Size Crochet,* and six other books. She designs knit and crochet projects for yarn companies and magazines and teaches at yarn shops, retreats, and national gatherings.

⦀ Tips and Tricks

Do not be afraid to make adjustments to the body or sleeve length of the garment. Take a moment to properly measure the person that the sweater will be made for and check the measurements against the chart. The measurements in the project specs are the finished measurements of the garment, not body measurements, so allow for wearing ease.

Man's Size	Small	Medium	Large	X-Large	XX-Large
Chest	34"–36" (86–91.5 cm)	38"–40" (96.5–101.5 cm)	42"–44" (106.5–111.5 cm)	46"–48" (116.5–122 cm)	50"–52" (127–132 cm)
Center Back Neck to Cuff	32"–32½" (81–82.5 cm)	33"–33½" (83.5–85 cm)	34"–34½" (86.5–87.5 cm)	35"–35½" (89–90 cm)	36"–36½" (91.5–92.5 cm)
Back Hip Length	25"–25½" (63.5–64.5 cm)	26½"–26¾" (67.5–68 cm)	27"–27¼" (68.5–69 cm)	27½"–27¾" (69.5–70.5 cm)	28"–28½" (71–72.5 cm)
Cross Back (Shoulder to Shoulder)	15½"–16" (39.5–40.5 cm)	16½"–17" (42–43 cm)	17½"–18" (44.5–45.5 cm)	18"–18½" (45.5–47 cm)	18½"–19" (47–48 cm)
Sleeve Length to Underarm	18" (45.5 cm)	18½" (47 cm)	19½" (49.5 cm)	20" (50.5 cm)	20½" (52 cm)

from Standards & Guidelines for Crochet and Knitting/Craft Yarn Council of America

Another way to determine which size to make is to take the measurements of a garment that fits the person you are knitting for. Use these measurements as a goal for your project. Use the garment as a template for your work, and regularly check your knitted sections against it for fit.

There are several ways to change a garment to fit an individual size, and this can be accomplished by mixing pattern sizes.

■ If you need a "mixed" size—say you need an X-Large for chest measurement, but a Large for waist measurement—you can start out by making the Large size, gradually increase the extra stitches at the side seams, about 1" (2.5 cm) apart, until you reach the amount for the X-Large, then continue finishing as for X-Large.

■ Another "mixed" size trick—for example, if you need the width of an X-Large, but the body length would be too long—is to cast on stitches for X-Large, but follow lengths for Large or Medium. This makes a shorter, wider garment.

■ You can do this in reverse, casting on for the Small or Medium, and working lengths for Large or X-Large, to make a longer, narrower garment.

■ When making up the sleeves, if you need a longer sleeve, add one more even row between increases; if you need a shorter sleeve, make one less even row between increases.

There are also ways that you can change a neckline. If you love one of the sweaters that has a crewneck, you can very easily change it to a V-neck if you follow these steps.

1 Work until about 2" (5 cm) above the armhole shaping. Then divide the work in half vertically; if there are an uneven number of stitches, place the center stitch on a holder to be worked later for the center of the V.

2 Working each side with a separate ball of yarn, decrease 1 stitch on each side of the V every other row until you have the amount of stitches needed for the shoulder.

3 Work even on the remaining stitches until the piece measures the same length as the back to the shoulder. Bind off as instructed.

You can use another pattern's V-shaping border to finish your project.

Several of the garments have zipper closings. The tricky part is getting the two sides to match. Here's what I do:

1 First baste the two sides together. Place the zipper facedown on the wrong side, centering the teeth over the basted seam. Pin in place. Then hand-stitch the zipper to the sweater.

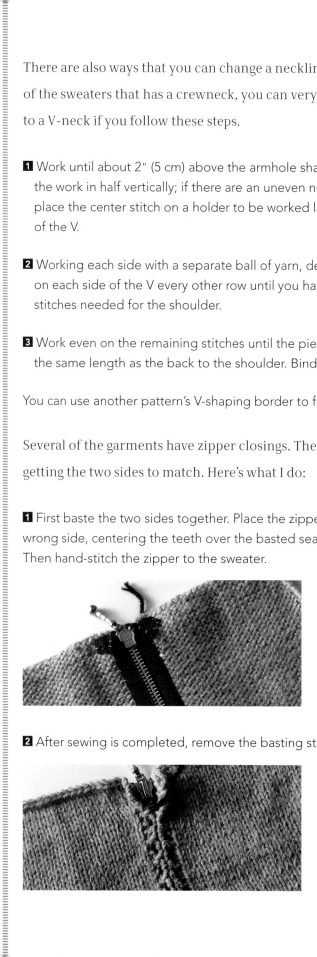

2 After sewing is completed, remove the basting stitches.

I have used the three-needle bind-off method on many of the garments. I love the look of this finish, and it looks especially great on dropped-shoulder garments. Directions for this technique are given on page 109.

When sewing tabs, such as the back neckband extensions on a cardigan, use the invisible weaving method of seaming, also called mattress stitch. This results in a smooth joint.

There's a special way to set in pockets that makes them blend smoothly with the sweater body. Here's what I do:

1 Place the pocket over the sweater front, aligning the stitch rows, and pin it in place.

2 With a tapestry needle, stitch the pocket in place using duplicate stitch. This means you stitch over the knit stitches on the outer edge of the pocket, echoing the path of the yarn and going through the sweater body with each stitch. I find this easier to do with a needle that has a curved tip.

Often you'll need to pick up stitches at a neckline or arm edge to add ribbing or a button band. You also need to pick up stitches when working the entrelac pattern (page 77). Using a crochet hook to pick up the stitches makes the job easier.

When you need to pick up a large number of stitches, estimate how many you need to pick up per side and pick them up evenly, closing all the gaps. If you get to the end and you've picked up a few too many or not quite enough, rather than start over, simply increase or decrease on the first row to the required number of stitches.

Always take the time to check your gauge. Change to different size needles if necessary to obtain the proper gauge.

YARN

Lightweight smooth yarn **3 LIGHT**

Shown: Suri Merino by Plymouth Yarn, 55% suri alpaca/45% extra-fine merino wool, 1.75 oz. (50 g)/110 yd. (100 m): #5297 blue, 19 (20, 21, 22) skeins

NEEDLES

Sizes 5 (3.75 mm) and 7 (4.5 mm) or sizes needed to obtain correct gauge

GAUGE

22 sts = 4" (10 cm) on size 7 needles in pat

Take time to check gauge.

NOTIONS

Two stitch holders

Tapestry needle

SIZES

Small (Medium, Large, X-Large)

Finished chest measurement: 44 (46, 48, 50)" [111.5 (116.5, 122, 127) cm]

Textured V-Neck Pullover

Soft, warm alpaca and wool-blend yarn knitted in a subtle textured stitch pattern gives this basic V-neck pullover unique style. Roomy enough to be worn comfortably over a long-sleeve shirt, this sweater works equally well for casual Fridays or out to dinner.

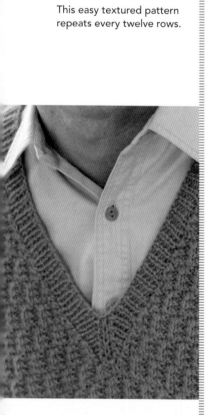

This easy textured pattern repeats every twelve rows.

Knit 1, purl 1 ribbing, worked on smaller needles, provides a snug fit at the sleeve ends, lower edge, and neckline. Neck ribbing is worked in one piece with decreases at the center front to form the V.

STITCH PATTERN

Multiple of 4 sts plus 3

Row 1: K3, *p1, k3, rep from * across row.

Row 2: K1, *p1, k3, rep from * to last 2 sts, p1, k1.

Rows 3 and 5: Rep Row 1.

Rows 4 and 6: Rep Row 2.

Rows 7, 9, and 11: Rep Row 2.

Rows 8, 10, and 12: Rep Row 1.

Rep Rows 1–12 for pat.

BACK

With size 5 needles, CO 122 (126, 134, 138) sts.

K1, p1 in rib for 2" (5 cm), inc 1 st at end of last row—123 (127, 135, 139) sts.

Change to size 7 needles. Work in pat until piece measures 14½ (15, 15½, 16)" [37 (38, 39.5, 40.5) cm] from beg, ending with a WS row.

Shape armholes: At beg of next 2 rows, BO 4 sts. Cont to work in pat as established on 115 (119, 127, 131) sts until armhole measures 9 (9½, 10, 10½)" [23 (24, 25.5, 26.5) cm] from beg, ending with a WS row.

Shape shoulders: At beg of next 2 rows, BO 34 (36, 38, 40) sts. Place rem 47 (47, 51, 51) sts on holder to be worked later for neckline.

FRONT

Work same as back until piece measures 1" (2.5 cm) above armhole shaping, ending with a WS row—115 (119, 127, 131) sts.

Shape V-neck: Keeping pat as established, work across 54 (56, 60, 62) sts, k2tog, k1, place the next st on a holder to be worked later for center of V-neck, join a new ball of yarn and work rem 57 (59, 63, 65) sts as foll: k1, k2tog, work pat on rem 54 (56, 60, 62) sts.

Cont to work both right and left fronts at the same time, each with a separate ball of yarn, being sure to keep pat as established.

Row 1 (WS): Foll pat to last st before center, k1; on other side of V, k1, foll pat to end of row.

Row 2: Work pat to last 3 sts before center, k2tog (dec made), k1; on other side of V, k1, k2tog (dec made), foll pat to end of row.

Row 3: Rep Row 1.

Row 4: Rep Row 1.

Rep Rows 1–4 until 34 (36, 38, 40) sts rem on each side. Work even until armhole is same measurement as back to shoulder. BO rem 34 (36, 38, 40) sts each side.

SLEEVES

Make 2.

With size 5 needles, CO 50 (54, 58, 62) sts. K1, p1 in rib for 2" (5 cm), inc 1 st at end of last row—51 (55, 59, 63) sts.

Change to size 7 needles and work in pat. Inc 1 st each side on Row 6 and every foll 4th row 23 (24, 25, 26) times more, working inc sts into pat—99 (105, 111, 117) sts.

Cont in pat until sleeve measures 20 (20½, 21, 22)" [51 (52, 53.5, 56) cm] from beg. BO loosely.

NECKBAND

Sew left shoulder seam. With RS facing you, place the 47 (47, 51, 51) sts from back neck holder on size 5 needle and k these sts, pick up and k50 (52, 54, 56) sts down left side of V, place marker on needle, k center st from holder, place marker on needle, pick up and k50 (52, 54, 56) sts up right side of V—148 (152, 160, 164) sts.

Shape V-neck:

Row 1 (WS): K1, p1 in rib until 2 sts before first marker, k2tog through the back loop, sl marker, p center st, sl marker, sl next st, k1, pass the sl st over k st, p1, k1 in rib to end of row.

Row 2 (RS): K1, p1 in rib until 2 sts before first marker, sl next st, k1, pass the sl st over k st, sl marker, k center st, sl marker, k2tog through the front loop, p1, k1 in rib to end of row.

Rows 3, 5, and 7: Rep Row 1.

Rows 4 and 6: Rep Row 2.

Row 8: BO in rib, dec center as Row 2 while you are binding off.

FINISHING

Sew right shoulder seam.

Fold sleeve in half. Mark center of sleeve and pin to center of shoulder seam. Pin sleeve in place, then sew in sleeve. Sew underarm seams.

Blocking is not recommended for this pattern stitch.

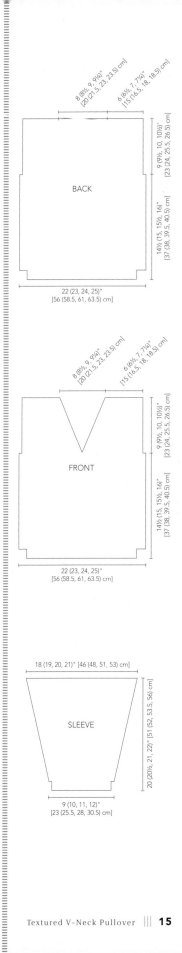
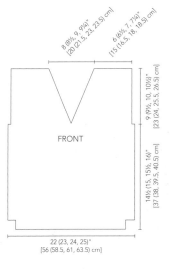

YARN

Lightweight smooth yarn

Shown: Baby Alpaca DK by Plymouth Yarn, 100% baby alpaca, 1.75 oz. (50 g)/125 yd. (115 m): (A) #208 Dark Tan, 7 (7, 8, 9) balls; (B) #207 Light Tan, 4 (4, 5, 6) balls; (C) #401 Gray, 2 (2, 3, 3) balls

NEEDLES

Sizes 3 (3.25 mm) and 6 (4 mm) or sizes needed to obtain correct gauge

GAUGE

22 sts = 4" (10 cm) on size 6 needles in St st

Take time to check gauge.

NOTIONS

Two stitch holders

Tapestry needle

SIZES

Small (Medium, Large, X-Large)

Finished chest measurement: 44 (46, 48, 50)"
[111.5 (116.5, 122, 127) cm]

Bold Striped Crewneck

This classic crewneck sweater is luxuriously soft, made in 100% alpaca yarn. The bold stripe pattern has long been a favorite for men of all ages. Knit one in subdued colors like these soft naturals, or choose a different color combo. The stripes are most effective if you use two contrasting values for the wide stripes and a medium value for the thin stripes.

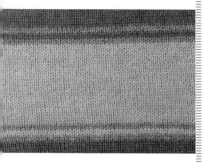

Plain and simple stockinette stitch (knit on right side, purl on wrong side) makes the knitting go quickly and creates an ultra-smooth fabric.

Knit 1, purl 1 ribbing at the cuffs, bottom, and neck gives a snug fit.

STRIPING PATTERN FOR FRONT AND BACK

28	rows color A
2	rows color C
2	rows color B
2	rows color C
28	rows color B
2	rows color C
2	rows color A
2	rows color C

BACK

With size 3 needles and color A, CO 120 (126, 132, 138) sts. K1, p1 in rib for 2½" (6.5 cm).

Change to size 6 needles. Work in St st (k on RS, p on WS) until 14½ (15, 15½, 16)" [37 (38, 39.5, 40.5) cm] from beg, foll striping pat throughout.

Shape armholes: At beg of next 2 rows, BO 7 sts—106 (112, 118, 124) sts. Cont in striping pat, keeping last stripe in color A, until armhole measures 9 (9½, 10, 10½)" [23 (24, 25.5, 26.5) cm].

Shape shoulders: At beg of next 2 rows, BO 34 (36, 38, 40) sts.

Place rem 38 (40, 42, 44) sts on a holder to be worked later for neckband.

FRONT

Work same as back until armhole measures 6 (6½, 7, 7½)" [15 (16.5, 18, 19) cm].

Shape neck: Work across 40 (42, 44, 46) sts, place center 26 (28, 30, 32) sts on holder (to be worked later for neckband), join new ball of yarn and work rem 40 (42, 44, 46) sts. Working both sides at the same time, each with a separate ball of yarn, dec 1 st at each neck edge every other row 6 times—34 (36, 38, 40) sts each side. Work even until same as back to shoulder.

Shape shoulders: Beg at armhole side, BO rem 34 (36, 38, 40) sts.

STRIPING PATTERN FOR SLEEVES

2	rows color C
2	rows color B
2	rows color C
28	rows color B
2	rows color C
2	rows color A
2	rows color C
28	rows color A

SLEEVES

Make 2.

With size 3 needles and A, CO 48 (50, 52, 54) sts. K1, p1 in rib for 3" (7.5 cm), ending with a WS row.

Next row (RS): Join C, k, inc 10 sts evenly spaced—58 (60, 62, 64) sts.

Change to size 6 needles. Work in St st, foll sleeve striping pat throughout, inc 1 st each side on 4th row, then every 4th row 20 (22, 24, 26) times more—100 (106, 112, 118) sts.

Work even until sleeve measures 20½ (21, 22, 22½)" [52 (53.5, 56, 57) cm] from beg. BO loosely.

NECKBAND

Sew left shoulder seam. With RS facing, place the 38 (40, 42, 44) sts from back neck holder onto size 3 needle and k these sts, pick up and k24 sts along left neck edge, sl 26 (28, 30, 32) sts from front neck holder onto needle and k these sts, pick up and k24 sts along right front neck edge—112 (116, 120, 124) sts.

K1, p1 in rib for 1" (2.5 cm). BO in pat.

FINISHING

Sew right shoulder and neckband seam.

Fold sleeve in half. Mark center of sleeve and pin to center of shoulder seam. Pin sleeve in place, then sew in sleeve. Sew underarm seams.

To block, lay sweater on a bath towel, spritz with water, and pat into shape.

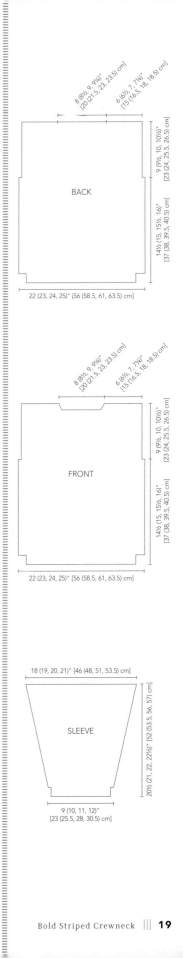

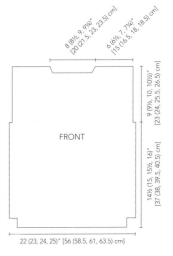

8 (8½, 9, 9¼)" [20 (21.5, 23, 23.5) cm]   6 (6½, 7, 7¼)" [15 (16.5, 18, 18.5) cm]

9 (9½, 10, 10½)" [23 (24, 25.5, 26.5) cm]

BACK

14½ (15, 15½, 16)" [37 (38, 39.5, 40.5) cm]

22 (23, 24, 25)" [56 (58.5, 61, 63.5) cm]

8 (8½, 9, 9¼)" [20 (21.5, 23, 23.5) cm]   6 (6½, 7, 7¼)" [15 (16.5, 18, 18.5) cm]

9 (9½, 10, 10½)" [23 (24, 25.5, 26.5) cm]

FRONT

14½ (15, 15½, 16)" [37 (38, 39.5, 40.5) cm]

22 (23, 24, 25)" [56 (58.5, 61, 63.5) cm]

18 (19, 20, 21)" [46 (48, 51, 53.5) cm]

SLEEVE

20½ (21, 22, 22½)" [52 (53.5, 56, 57) cm]

9 (10, 11, 12)" [23 (25.5, 28, 30.5) cm]

YARN

Lightweight smooth yarn

Shown: Alpaca Silk DK by Debbie Bliss, 80% baby alpaca/20% silk, 1.75 oz. (50 g)/115 yd. (105 m): #26009 Teal, 13 (14, 15, 16) balls

NEEDLES

Sizes 4 (3.5 mm) and 6 (4 mm) or sizes needed to obtain correct gauge

Size 4 (3.5 mm) circular needle, 24" (61 cm) long for neckband

GAUGE

22 sts = 4" (10 cm) on size 6 needles in pat

Take time to check gauge.

NOTIONS

Large stitch holder

Three small stitch holders

Tapestry needle

SIZES

Small (Medium, Large, X-Large)

Finished chest measurement: 44 (46, 48, 50)" [111.5 (116.5, 122, 127) cm]

Rib-Stitch Pullover

Casual elegance only begins to describe this handsome sweater. Knitted from a blended yarn of alpaca and silk, it is also a treat to wear. A combination of rib widths gives the sweater interesting style while hugging him ever so slightly.

The rib pattern changes at mid-chest.

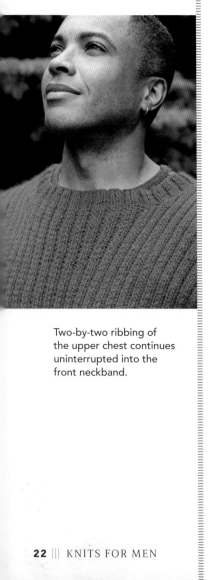

Two-by-two ribbing of the upper chest continues uninterrupted into the front neckband.

BACK

With size 4 needles, CO 124 (128, 132, 136) sts. K1, p1 in rib for 2½" (6.5 cm), ending with a WS row.

Change to size 6 needles. Work first rib pat as foll:

Row 1 (RS): P11 (13, 15, 17), *k2, p2, k2, p6, rep from * 8 times more, end p5 (7, 9, 11).

Row 2: K11 (13, 15, 17), *p2, k2, p2, k6, rep from * 8 times more, end k5 (7, 9, 11).

Rep Rows 1 and 2 until 12½ (13, 13½, 14)" [31.5 (33, 34.5, 35.5) cm] from beg, ending with a WS row.

Beg second rib pat as foll:

Row 1 (RS): For sizes Small and Large: K1, *p2, k2, rep from * across row to last 3 sts, p2, k1.

For sizes Medium and X-Large: P1, k2, *p2, k2, rep from * across row to last st, p1.

Row 2: For sizes Small and Large: P1, *k2, p2, rep from * across row to last 3 stst, k2, p1.

For sizes Medium and X-Large: K1, p2, *k2, p2, rep from * across row to last st, end k1.

Rep Rows 1 and 2 until piece measures 15 (15½, 16, 16½)" [38 (39.5, 40.5, 42) cm] from beg.

Shape armholes: At beg of next 2 rows, BO 5 sts. Keeping second rib pat as established, work until armhole is 9 (9½, 10, 10½)" [23 (24, 25.5, 26.5) cm].

Place rem 114 (118, 122, 126) sts on holder to be worked later.

FRONT

Work same as back until armhole is 6½ (7, 7½, 8)" [16.5 (18, 19, 20.5) cm], end with a WS row.

Shape neck: Cont in pat as established, work across 38 (40, 42, 44) sts, place center 38 sts on holder (to be worked later for neckband), join new ball of yarn and work rem 38 (40, 42, 44) sts.

Working both sides at the same time, each with a separate ball of yarn, cont in pat as established, dec 1 st at each neck edge every other row 6 times— 32 (34, 36, 38) sts each side.

Holding front and back RS together, using three-needle BO, BO 32 (34, 36, 38) sts of each shoulder together, leave 50 rem sts of back on holder to be worked for neckband.

SLEEVES

Make 2.

With size 4 needles, CO 50 (54, 58, 62) sts. K1, p1 in rib for 2½" (6.5 cm), ending with a RS row. On next row, k, inc 12 sts evenly across row—62 (66, 70, 74) sts.

Change to size 6 needles. Work sleeve rib pat as foll:

Row 1 (RS): P4 (6, 8, 10), *k2, p2, k2, p6, rep from * 3 times more, end k2, p2, k2, p4 (6, 8, 10).

Row 2: K4 (6, 8, 10), *p2, k2, p2, k6, rep from * 3 times more, end p2, k2, p2, k4 (6, 8, 10).

Rep Rows 1 and 2 for sleeve rib pat and at same time, inc 1 st each side every 6th row 20 times, keeping inc sts in rev St st. Work even, keeping pat as established on 102 (106, 110, 114) sts until sleeve is 20½ (2l, 22, 22½)" [52 (53.5, 56, 57) cm] from beg. BO loosely.

NECKBAND

Using size 4 circular needle, with RS facing you and starting at right shoulder, foll rib on back of neck working across 50 sts, pick up 20 sts along dec edge of left side, foll rib on center 38 sts, pick up 20 sts along dec edge of right side—128 sts. Work in p2, k2 rib for 1½" (4 cm). BO loosely in rib pat.

FINISHING

Fold sleeve in half. Mark center of sleeve and pin to center of shoulder seam. Pin sleeve in place, then sew in sleeve. Sew underarm seams.

Blocking is not recommended for this rib pattern.

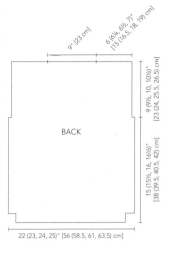

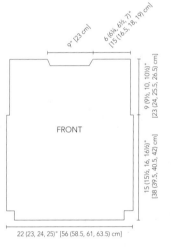

YARN

Medium-weight smooth yarn **4 MEDIUM**

Shown: Washable Wool by Moda Dea, 100% merino wool, 3.5 oz. (100 g)/166 yd. (152 m): #4440 Moss, 9 (9, 10, 10) skeins

NEEDLES

Sizes 5 (3.75 mm) and 8 (5 mm) or sizes needed to obtain correct gauge

GAUGE

19 sts = 4" (10 cm) on size 8 needles in pat

Take time to check gauge.

NOTIONS

Four buttons, ¾" (2 cm) diameter

Two stitch holders

Tapestry needle

SIZES

Small (Medium, Large, X-Large)

Finished chest measurement: 46 (48, 50, 52)" [116.5 (122, 127, 132) cm]

Nubby Pocket Cardigan

A deep V-neck, rib-top pockets, and a nubby stitch give this time-tested favorite lots of added interest. With its slightly loose fit, this is a great sweater for golfing or a walk in the park. The stitch pattern is very easy—just be sure to keep to the pattern as you increase and decrease stitches.

Nubby Stitch, also called Sand Stitch, can be used with either side facing out. For this sweater, I chose the bumpy side to face out and the smoother side to face in.

NUBBY STITCH

Worked on uneven number of sts

Row 1 (WS): K across row.

Row 2: K1, *p1, k1, rep from * across row.

Notes:

1 To coincide with the Nubby Stitch pattern, the ribbing is worked on an uneven number of stitches.

2 When binding off, always bind off in pattern.

BACK

With size 5 needles, CO 111 (115, 119, 123) sts.

Beg border as foll:

Row 1 (WS): K1, *p1, k1, rep from * across row.

Row 2: P1, *k1, p1, rep from * across row.

Rep border Rows 1 and 2 for 2" (5 cm), ending with an RS row.

Change to size 8 needles. Work Nubby St pat until back measures 14½ (15, 15½, 16)" [37 (38, 39.5, 40.5) cm] from beg, ending with a WS row.

Shape armholes: At beg of next 2 rows, BO 5 (5, 6, 6) sts. Work even, keeping pat as established on rem 101 (105, 107, 111) sts until armhole is 9½ (10, 10½, 11)" [24 (25.5, 26.5, 28) cm], ending with a WS row.

Shape shoulders: At beg of next 2 rows, BO 30 (32, 33, 35) sts. BO rem 41 (41, 41, 41) sts.

POCKET LININGS

Make 2 (before beg fronts).

With size 8 needles, CO 39 sts. Work Nubby St pat for 5" (12.5 cm), ending with a RS row. Place sts on holder.

RIGHT FRONT

With size 5 needles, CO 63 (65, 67, 69) sts.

Beg border as foll:

Row 1 (RS): K1, *p1, k1, rep from * across row.

Row 2: *P1, k1, rep from * to last 9 sts, p1, k8.

Rep Rows 1 and 2 until border is 2" (5 cm), ending with a WS row.

Change to size 8 needles. Beg body pat as foll:

Row 1: K1, *p1, k1, rep from * across row.

Row 2: K to last 9 sts, p1, k8.

Rep last 2 rows until 7" (18 cm) from beg, ending with a RS row.

Set in pocket as foll:

Next row (WS): Work pat on 6 sts, BO next 39 sts, foll pat to end of row.

Next row (RS): Work pat to BO sts, work sts from pocket lining, keeping pat as established in place of BO sts, cont pat to end of row.

Cont pat as established until 12½ (13, 13½, 14)" [31.5 (33, 34.5, 35.5) cm] from beg, ending with a WS row.

Shape V-neck:

First dec row (RS): K1, *p1, k1, rep from * 3 times more, sl1, k1, psso (dec made), **p1, k1, rep from ** to end of row.

Cont in pat, dec neck edge in this manner on 4th row two times more, then every other row, always making dec after first 9 border sts; AT THE SAME TIME, when piece is 14½ (15, 15½, 16)" [37 (38, 39.5, 40.5) cm] from beg, BO 5 (5, 6, 6) sts at arm edge. Cont in this manner, keeping pat as established and cont neck dec every other row until 38 (40, 41, 43) sts rem. Work even in pat until armhole is 9½ (10, 10½, 11)" [24 (25.5, 26.5, 28) cm].

Shape shoulder: Beg at arm edge, BO 30 (32, 33, 35) sts, cont in pat on rem 8 border sts for 3½ (3½, 4, 4)" [9 (9, 10, 10) cm] more for neckband extension. BO.

Using size 5 needles, with RS facing you, pick up 39 sts along BO edges of pocket. K1, p1 in rib for 4 rows, BO in rib.

LEFT FRONT

Before beg left front, using pins, mark right front as a guide for four buttonholes, having 1st buttonhole about ½" (1.3 cm) up from bottom and 4th one just below beg of V-shaping.

With size 5 needles, CO 63 (65, 67, 69) sts.

Beg border as foll:

Row 1 (RS): K1, *p1, k1, rep from * across row.

Row 2: K8, p1, *k1, p1, rep from * across row.

Rep Row 1 once more.

To make 1st buttonhole, with WS facing, k3, BO next 2 sts, k3, (p1, k1) to end of row.

Rep Row 2, CO 2 sts over BO sts (buttonhole completed).

Cont rep Rows 1 and 2 of border pat until border is 2" (5 cm), ending with a WS row.

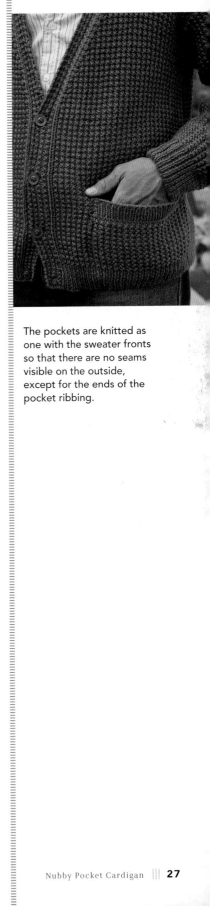

The pockets are knitted as one with the sweater fronts so that there are no seams visible on the outside, except for the ends of the pocket ribbing.

Pocket linings are knitted separately and then knitted together with the sweater fronts. The sides and bottom of the pocket linings are sewn to the wrong side.

Change to size 8 needles. Beg body pat as foll:

Row 1: K1, *p1, k1, rep from * across row.

Row 2: K8, p1, k to end of row.

Rep last 2 rows until 7" (18 cm) from beg, making buttonholes as before, using right front markers as guide, ending with an RS row.

Set in pocket as foll:

Next row (WS): Work pat on 18 (20, 22, 24) sts, BO next 39 sts, work pat on rem 6 sts.

Next row (RS): Work pat up to BO sts, foll pat work sts from pocket lining, cont pat to end of row.

Cont pat as established until 12½ (13, 13½, 14)" [31.5 (33, 34.5, 35.5) cm] from beg, end with a WS row.

Shape V-neck:

First dec row (RS): *K1, p1, rep from * until 11 sts from front edge, k2tog from front loop, k1, **p1, k1, rep from ** across row.

Cont in pat, dec neck edge in this manner on 4th row two times more, then every other row, always making dec before first 9 border sts and AT THE SAME TIME, when piece is 14½ (15, 15½, 16)" [37 (38, 39.5, 40.5) cm] from beg, BO 5 (5, 6, 6) sts at arm edge. Cont in this manner, keeping pat as established and cont neck dec every other row until 38 (40, 41, 43) sts rem. Work even in pat until armhole is 9½ (10, 10½, 11)" [24 (25.5, 26.5, 28) cm].

Shape shoulder: Beg at arm edge, BO 30 (32, 33, 35) sts, cont in pat on rem 8 border sts for 3½ (3½, 4, 4)" [9 (9, 10, 10) cm] more for neckband extension. BO.

Using size 5 needles, with RS facing you, pick up 39 sts along BO edges of pocket. K1, p1 in rib for 4 rows. BO in rib.

SLEEVES

Make 2.

With size 5 needles, CO 51 (53, 55, 57) sts. Work in k1, p1 rib for 3" (7.5 cm).

Change to size 8 needles. Work pat as back, inc 1 st each side on 1st row, then rep inc every 4th row, keep pat as sts are increased, until you have 91 (95, 99, 103) sts. Work even until sleeve is 20½ (21, 21½, 22)" [52 (53.5, 54.5, 56) cm] from beg. BO in pat.

FINISHING

Sew pocket linings in place on WS of front pieces. Sew ends of pocket ribbing in place on RS.

Sew shoulder seams.

Fold sleeve in half. Mark center of sleeve and pin to center of shoulder seam. Pin sleeve in place, then sew in sleeve. Sew underarm seams.

Sew ends of band extensions together, pin seam at center back, and sew in place.

Blocking is not recommended for this pattern stitch.

Sew on buttons opposite buttonholes.

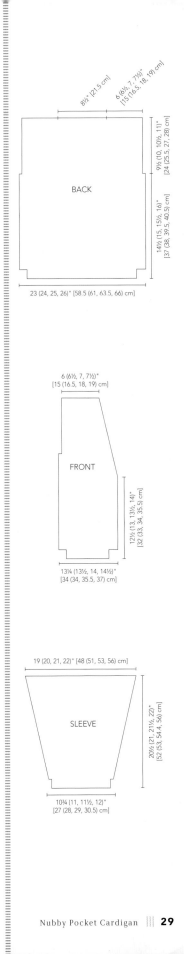

YARN

Medium-weight smooth yarn ![4 MEDIUM]

Shown: Ultra Alpaca by Berroco, 50% alpaca/50% wool, 3.5 oz. (100 g)/215 yd. (198 m): (MC) #6229 Sweet Potato, 7 (7, 8, 8) skeins; (CC) #6201 Cream, 1 skein

NEEDLES

Sizes 5 (3.75 mm) and 8 (5 mm) or sizes needed to obtain correct gauge

Cable needle

GAUGE

20 sts = 4" (10 cm) on size 8 needles in St st

Take time to check gauge.

NOTIONS

Two stitch holders

Tapestry needle

SIZES

Small (Medium, Large, X-Large)

Finished chest measurement: 44 (46, 48, 50)" [111.5 (116.5, 122, 127) cm]

Chunky Cabled Pullover

Large cables give this pullover a handsome, rugged look. Knitted from wonderfully plush alpaca yarn, this warm and cozy sweater will take the chill out of winter in a stylish way. Although they offer texture and interest to a sweater, cables also tend to draw in the knitted fabric, but this has already been accommodated in the stitch count and sizing.

Reverse stockinette stitch provides a recessed background that makes the cable columns stand out.

BACK

With size 5 needles, CO 112 (116, 120, 124) sts.

Beg waistband as foll:

Row 1: *K1, p1, rep from * across row. Rep Row 1 for 2" (5 cm), ending with a WS row.

Next row: K, inc 6 (8, 10, 12) sts evenly spaced across row—118 (124, 130, 136) sts.

Next row: P across row.

Change to size 8 needles. Beg cable pat as foll:

Row 1 (RS): P11 (14, 17, 20), k6, p10, *k5, p1, k6, p3, k6, p1, k5, p10, rep from * once more, k6, p11 (14, 17, 20).

Row 2: K11 (14, 17, 20), p6, k10, *p5, k1, p6, k3, p6, k1, p5, k10, rep from * once more, p6, k11 (14, 17, 20).

Row 3: P11 (14, 17, 20), sl next 3 sts to a cable needle, hold to front of work, k next 3 sts, k3 from cable needle (cable twist made), p10, *k5, p1, sl next 3 sts to cable needle, hold in back of work, k next 3, k3 from cable needle, p3, sl next 3 sts to cable needle, hold in front of work, k next 3, k3 from cable needle, p1, k5, p10, rep from * once more, sl next 3 sts to cable needle, hold in front of work, k next 3, k3 from cable needle, p11 (14, 17, 20).

Row 4: Rep Row 2.

Row 5: Rep Row 1.

Row 6: Rep Row 2.

Row 7: Rep Row 3.

Row 8: Rep Row 2.

Row 9: Rep Row 1.

Row 10: Rep Row 2.

Row 11: P11 (14, 17, 20), k6, p10, *sl next 6 sts to cable needle, hold in front of work, k next 6 sts, k6 from cable needle, p3, sl next 6 sts to cable needle hold in back of work, k next 6 sts, k6 from cable needle, p10, rep from * once more, k6, p11 (14, 17, 20).

Row 12: K11 (14, 17, 20), p6, k10, *p6, k1, p5, k3, p5, k1, p6, k10, rep from * once more, p6, k11 (14, 17, 20).

Row 13: P11 (14, 17, 20), k6, p10, *k6, p1, k5, p3, k5, p1, k6, p10, rep from * once more, k6, p11 (14, 17, 20).

Row 14: Rep Row 12.

Row 15: P11 (14, 17, 20), k6, p10, *sl next 3 sts onto cable needle and hold to front of work, k next 3 sts, k3 from cable needle, p1, k5, p3, k5, p1, sl next 3 sts to cable needle and hold to back of work, k next 3 sts, k3 from cable needle, p10, rep from * once more, k6, p11 (14, 17, 20).

Row 16: Rep Row 12.

Row 17: Rep Row 13.

Row 18: Rep Row 12.

Row 19: Rep Row 15.

Row 20: Rep Row 12.

Row 21: Rep Row 13.

Row 22: Rep Row 12.

Row 23: P11 (14, 17, 20), sl next 3 sts onto cable needle and hold to front of work, k next 3 sts, k3 from cable needle, p10, *sl next 3 sts onto cable needle and hold to front of work, k next 3, k3 from cable needle, p1, k5, p3, k5, p1, sl next 3 sts to cable needle and hold to back of work, k next 3 sts, k3 from cable needle, p10, rep from * once more, sl next 3 sts to cable needle and hold to front of work, k next 3 sts, k3 from cable needle, p11 (14, 17, 20).

Row 24: Rep Row 12.

Row 25: Rep Row 13.

Row 26: Rep Row 12.

Row 27: Rep Row 23.

Row 28: Rep Row 12.

Row 29: Rep Row 13.

Row 30: Rep Row 12.

Row 31: P11 (14, 17, 20), k6, p10, *sl next 6 sts to cable needle and hold to back of work, k next 6 sts, k6 from cable needle, p3, sl next 6 sts to cable needle and hold to front of work, k next 6 sts, k6 from cable needle, p10, rep from * once more, k6, p11 (14, 17, 20).

Row 32: Rep Row 2.

Row 33: Rep Row 1.

Row 34: Rep Row 2.

Row 35: P11 (14, 17, 20), k6, p10, *k5, p1, sl next 3 sts to cable needle and hold in back of work, k next 3 sts, k3 from cable needle, p3, sl next 3 sts to cable needle and hold in front of work, k next 3 sts, k3 from cable needle, p1, k5, p10, rep from * once more, k6, p11 (14, 17, 20).

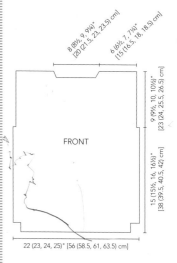

Row 36: Rep Row 2.

Row 37: Rep Row 1.

Row 38: Rep Row 2.

Row 39: Rep Row 35.

Row 40: Rep Row 2.

Rep Rows 1–40 for cable pat.

Work in pat until piece measures 15 (15½, 16, 16½)" [38 (39.5, 40.5, 42) cm] from beg, ending with a WS row.

Shape armholes: At beg of next 2 rows BO 4 sts—110 (116, 122, 128) sts. Cont in pat as established until armhole measures 9 (9½, 10, 10½)" [23 (24, 25.5, 26.5) cm].

Shape shoulder: At beg of next 2 rows, BO 32 (34, 36, 38) sts, place rem 46 (48, 50, 52) sts on a holder to be worked later for neckband.

FRONT

Work same as back until armhole measures 7 (7½, 8, 8½)" [18 (19, 20.5, 21.5) cm].

Shape neck: Being sure to keep pat as established, work across 37 (40, 43, 46) sts, place center 36 sts on a holder, join a new ball of yarn and work rem 37 (40, 43, 46) sts. Working both sides at once, each on a separate ball of yarn, keeping pat as established, dec 1 st at each neck edge every row 5 (6, 7, 8) times—32 (34, 36, 38) sts each side. Work even until armhole measures 9 (9½, 10, 10½)" [23 (24, 25.5, 26.5) cm].

Shape shoulders: At beg of next 2 rows, BO 32 (34, 36, 38) sts.

SLEEVES

Make 2.

Note: Do not break yarn at the end of color changes; instead, carry it loosely up sides.

Sleeve border: With size 5 needles and MC, CO 44 (46, 48, 50) sts.

Rows 1–4: K1, p1 in rib as back.

Row 5: With CC, k across row.

Row 6: With CC, k1, p1 in rib.

Row 7: With MC, k across row.

Rows 8–10: With MC, k1, p1 in rib.

Rows 11–16: Rep Rows 5–10 once.

Next row: K, inc 10 sts evenly across row—54 (56, 58, 60) sts.

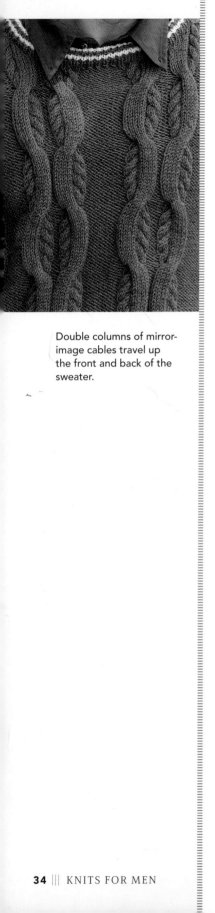

Double columns of mirror-image cables travel up the front and back of the sweater.

Next row: P across row.

Change to size 8 needles. Work cable pat for sleeves as foll; AT THE SAME TIME you are working cable pat, beg on the 4th row and cont inc 1 st each side every 4th row 18 (19, 20, 21) times—90 (94, 98 102) sts. Work even until sleeve measures 20½ (21, 21½, 22)" [52 (53.5, 54.5, 56) cm]. BO in pat.

Cable pat for sleeves:

Row 1 (RS): P11 (12, 13, 14), k6, p20, k6, p11 (12, 13, 14).

Row 2: K11 (12, 13, 14), p6, k20, p6, k11 (12, 13, 14).

Row 3: P11 (12, 13, 14), *sl next 3 sts to cable needle, hold to front of work, k next 3 sts, k3 from cable needle (cable twist made)*, p 20, rep from * to * once more, p11 (12, 13, 14).

Rows 4 and all even rows: Rep Row 2.

Rows 5: Rep Row 1.

Row 7: Rep Row 3 (cable twist row).

Rows 9, 11, 13, 15, 17, and 19: Rep Row 1.

Row 18: Rep Row 2.

Row 19: Rep Row 1.

Row 20: Rep Row 2.

Rep Rows 1–20 for sleeve cable pat.

NECKBAND

Sew left shoulder seam. Using MC and size 5 needles, with RS facing you, k46 (48, 50, 52) from back neck holder, pick up and k14 sts along left front neck shaping, k36 sts from front neck holder, then pick up and k14 sts along right neck shaping—110 (112, 114, 116) sts. With size 5 needles, work neckband same as sleeve border. After last CC stripe is worked, work 1" (2.5 cm) with MC in rib. BO loosely.

FINISHING

Sew right shoulder and neckband seam. Fold neckband to inside and sew down. Fold sleeve in half. Mark center of sleeve and pin to center of shoulder seam. Pin sleeve in place, then sew in sleeve. Sew underarm seams.

To block, lay sweater on a bath towel, spray with water, and pat into shape.

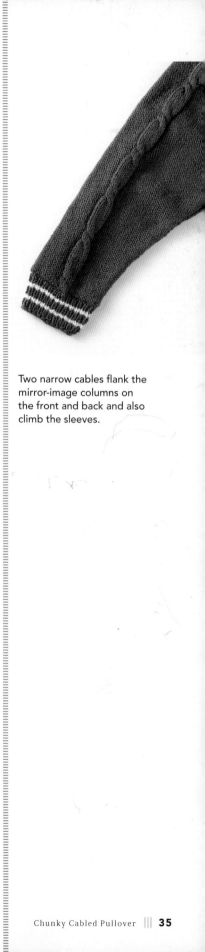

Two narrow cables flank the mirror-image columns on the front and back and also climb the sleeves.

YARN

Medium-weight smooth wool

Shown: Aussie Wool, worsted weight, 100% premium Australian wool, 200 yd. (184 m)/3.5 oz. (100 g): WW 53 Commodore, 10 (10, 11, 11) skeins

NEEDLES

Sizes 5 (3.75 mm) and 8 (5 mm) or sizes needed to obtain correct gauge

GAUGE

20 sts = 4" (10 cm) on size 8 needles in st pat

Take time to check gauge.

NOTIONS

Six stitch holders

Tapestry needle

4½" (11.5 cm) leather/wood toggle

SIZES

Small (Medium, Large, X-Large)

Finished chest measurement:
44 (46, 48, 50)"
[111.5 (116.5, 122, 127) cm]

Toggle Collar Pullover

This casual sweater has a collar with a unique toggle closure. Worsted-weight wool worked up in a basket-weave stitch pattern makes this sweater warm and rugged. Look for a leather and wood toggle closure in the button department of a fabric store or yarn shop or check online at www.mjtrim.com.

Alternating blocks of knit and purl stitches set up a pattern that resembles woven strips—thus the name "basket weave."

A leather and wood toggle closure is sewn in place by hand.

BASKET WEAVE

Multiple of 8 sts plus 3

Row 1 (RS): K across row.

Row 2: K4, p3, *k5, p3, rep from * to last 4 sts, k4.

Row 3: P4, k3, *p5, k3, rep from * to last 4 sts, p4.

Row 4: Rep Row 2.

Row 5: K across row.

Row 6: P3, *k5, p3, rep from * across row.

Row 7: K3, *p5, k3, rep from * across row.

Row 8: Rep Row 6.

Rep Rows 1–8 for pat.

BACK

With size 5 needles, CO 110 (114, 120, 124) sts. K1, p1 in rib for 2½" (6.5 cm), inc 1 st at end of last row—111 (115, 121, 125) sts.

Change to size 8 needles and work as foll:

Row 1: K2 (0, 3, 1), place marker on needle, work pat Row 1 to last 2 (0, 3, 1) sts, place marker on needle, k last 2 (0, 3, 1) sts.

Row 2: P2 (0, 3, 1), sl marker, work pat Row 2 to last 2 (0, 3, 1) sts, sl marker, p last 2 (0, 3, 1) sts.

Cont, keeping 2 (0, 3, 1) sts in St st on each side and work pat rows in center until piece measures 15 (15½, 16, 16½)" [38 (39.5, 40.5, 42) cm] from beg, ending with a WS row.

Shape armhole: At beg of next 2 rows, BO 7 sts, being sure to keep pat as established on center 97 (101, 107, 111) sts. Cont until armhole is 9 (9½, 10, 10½)" [23 (24, 25.5, 26.5) cm].

Shape shoulder: Work 30 (31, 32, 33) sts and place sts on a holder for right shoulder, BO center 37 (39, 43, 45) sts, work rem 30 (31, 32, 33) sts and place sts on a holder for left shoulder.

FRONT

Work same as back until armhole is 2 (2½, 3, 3½)" [5 (6.5, 7.5, 9) cm], ending with a WS row.

Divide for front opening:

Left front: Work 48 (50, 53, 55) sts, place rem 49 (51, 54, 56) sts on holder to be worked later for right front.

Being sure to keep pat as established, work until armhole is 7 (7½, 8, 8½)" [18 (19, 20.5, 21.5) cm], ending at arm side.

Shape shoulder: Work 34 (36, 38, 40) sts, place rem 14 (14, 15, 15) sts on holder to be worked later for collar. Cont as established on rem 34 (36, 38, 40) sts, dec 1 st at neck edge, every row 4 (5, 6, 7) times—30 (31, 32, 33) sts. Work even until piece measures same as back to shoulder. Place rem sts on holder.

Right front: Join yarn at center front, BO 1 st, then work 48 (50, 53, 55) sts, being sure to keep pat as established. Work until armhole is 7 (7½, 8, 8½)" [18 (19, 20.5, 21.5) cm], ending at neck edge.

Shape shoulder: Work 14 (14, 15, 15) sts and place them on holder to be worked later for collar, then cont pat on rem 34 (36, 38, 40) sts. Cont pat dec 1 st at neck edge every row 4 (5, 6, 7) times. Work even on rem 30 (31, 32, 33) sts until piece measures same as back to shoulder. Place rem sts on holder.

SLEEVES

Make 2.

With size 5 needles, CO 54 (56, 58, 60) sts. K1, p1 in rib for 2½" (6.5 cm). K, inc 5 (3, 9, 7) sts evenly across row—59 (59, 67, 67) sts. Change to size 8 needles. Beg with pat Row 2 and work in pat, and at the same time, inc 1 st each side on 4th row, then every 8th row 15 (17, 16, 17) times more, being sure to keep inc sts in pat as established—91 (95, 101, 103) sts. Work even until sleeve measures 21 (21½, 22, 22½)" [53.5 (54.5, 56, 57) cm] from beg. BO loosely.

COLLAR

Slip right front and back shoulder sts from holders onto separate needles with RS together. Join shoulders using three-needle BO method. Join left front and back shoulders in the same manner.

Using size 5 needles, with RS facing you and starting at right front, k14 (14, 15, 15) sts from right front holder, pick up and k17 (16, 17, 16) sts along right front neck decs, k37 (39, 43, 45) sts from back neck, pick up and k17 (16, 17, 16) sts along left front neck decs, then k14 (14, 15, 15) sts from left front holder—99 (99, 107, 107) sts.

Beg Basket Weave pat with Row 1 (this reverses collar) and work for 1" (2.5 cm). Change to size 8 needles and work for 3" (7.5 cm) more. BO loosely.

FINISHING

Fold sleeve in half. Mark center of sleeve and pin to center of shoulder seam. Pin sleeve in place, then sew in sleeve. Sew underarm seams. Sew on toggle closure.

Blocking is not recommended for this stitch pattern.

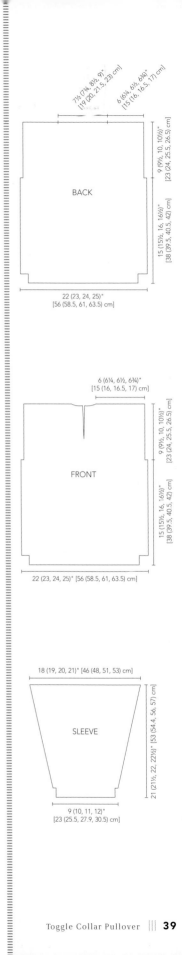

YARN

Medium-weight wool ④ MEDIUM

Shown: Nature Spun Worsted by Brown Sheep Company, 100% wool, 3.5 oz. (100 g)/245 yd. (224 m): #016 Burnt Sienna, 6 (7, 7, 8) skeins

NEEDLES

Sizes 5 (3.75 mm) and 7 (4.5 mm) or sizes needed to obtain correct gauge

Size 5 (3.75 mm) circular or double-pointed needles

GAUGE

20 sts = 4" (10 cm) on size 7 needles in pat

Take time to check gauge.

NOTIONS

Two stitch holders

Tapestry needle

SIZES

Small (Medium, Large, X-Large)

Finished chest measurement: 44 (46, 48, 50)" [111.5 (116.5, 122, 127) cm]

Windowpane Checks

Casual, comfortable, and versatile, this wool pullover will be the sweater he keeps at the top of the stack. The simple windowpane stitch pattern is easy to knit, and it gives the sweater just the right amount of textural interest.

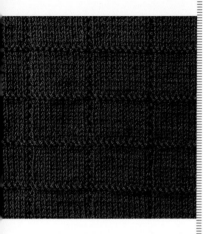

The stitch pattern is basically stockinette stitch. The windowpane effect is created by knitting on the wrong side in complete rows to make the horizontal bars and in every tenth stitch to make the vertical bars.

The neckband is turned to the inside and hand-stitched to create a neat, double-layer finish.

BACK

With size 5 needles, CO 102 (106, 110, 114) sts. K1, p1 in rib for 2½" (6.5 cm), ending with an RS row.

Next row (WS): K, inc 11 sts evenly spaced across row—113 (117, 121, 125) sts.

Next row (RS): K across row.

Change to size 7 needles. Work pat as foll:

Row 1 (WS): P1 (3, 5, 7), *k1, p10, rep from * 9 times more, end k1, p1 (3, 5, 7).

Row 2: K across row.

Rows 3, 5, 7, and 9: Rep Row 1.

Rows 4, 6, 8, and 10: Rep Row 2.

Rows 11 and 12: K across row.

Rep pat Rows 1–12 until back is 16" (40.5 cm) from beg, ending with a WS row.

Shape armholes: At beg of next 2 rows, BO 5 sts. Being sure to keep pat as established, cont on 103 (107, 111, 115) sts, until armhole is 9 (9½, 10, 11)" [23 (24, 25.5, 28) cm].

Shape shoulders: At beg of next 2 rows, BO 32 (33, 34, 35) sts, place rem 39 (41, 43, 45) sts on holder.

FRONT

Work same as back until armhole is 7 (7½, 8, 8½)" [18 (19, 20.5, 21.5) cm], ending with a WS row.

Shape neck: Work 40 (41, 42, 43) sts, sl center 23 (25, 27, 29) sts on holder, join new ball of yarn and work rem 40 (41, 42, 43) sts. Working both sides at the same time, each with a separate ball of yarn, dec 1 st at each neck edge every other row 8 times—32 (33, 34, 35) sts each side. Work same as back to shoulder. BO rem sts each side.

SLEEVES

Make 2.

With size 5 needles, CO 50 (54, 58, 62) sts. Work k1, p1 in rib for 2½" (6.5 cm), ending with an RS row.

Next row (WS): K, inc 16 (12, 8, 4) sts evenly spaced across row—66 sts.

Next row (RS): K across row.

Change to size 7 needles. Work pat as foll; AT THE SAME TIME, work inc sts and keep these sts in pat.

Row 1 (WS): P5, *k1, p10, rep from * 4 times more, end k1, p5.

Row 2: K across row.

Rows 3, 5, 7, and 9: Rep Row 1.

Rows 4, 6, 8, and 10: Rep Row 2.

Rows 11 and 12: K across row.

Rep pat Rows 1–12; AT THE SAME TIME, inc 1 st each side every 4th row 13 (15, 17, 19) times—92 (96, 100, 104) sts. Work even until sleeve is 21 (21½, 22, 22½)" [53.5 (54.5, 56, 57) cm] from beg. BO loosely.

NECKBAND

Sew shoulder seams.

Using circ or dp needles, with RS facing you and starting at back neck, k39 (41, 43, 45) sts from holder, pick up and k22 (23, 24, 25) sts along left front dec edge, k23 (25, 27, 29) sts from front neck holder, then pick up and k22 (23, 24, 25) sts along right front dec edge—106 (112, 118, 124) sts. Mark end of row. Join and k every rnd for 1" (2.5 cm). P 1 rnd for a turning ridge. K every rnd for ¾" (2 cm). BO in k.

FINISHING

Fold sleeve in half. Mark center of sleeve and pin to center of shoulder seam. Pin sleeve in place, then sew in sleeve. Sew underarm seams.

Turn neckband to inside and sew down.

If blocking is needed, spread garment on towels, spritz with water, hand press into desired shape, cover with towels, and allow to dry.

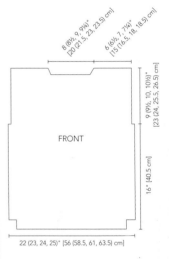

8 (8½, 9, 9¼)" [20 (21.5, 23, 23.5) cm]
6 (6½, 7, 7¼)" [15 (16.5, 18, 18.5) cm]
9 (9½, 10, 10½)" [23 (24, 25.5, 26.5) cm]
16" [40.5 cm]
BACK
22 (23, 24, 25)" [56 (58.5, 61, 63.5) cm]

8 (8½, 9, 9¼)" [20 (21.5, 23, 23.5) cm]
6 (6½, 7, 7¼)" [15 (16.5, 18, 18.5) cm]
9 (9½, 10, 10½)" [23 (24, 25.5, 26.5) cm]
16" [40.5 cm]
FRONT
22 (23, 24, 25)" [56 (58.5, 61, 63.5) cm]

18 (19, 20, 21)" [46 (48, 51, 53.5) cm]
21 (21½, 22, 22½)" [53 (54.5, 56, 57) cm]
SLEEVE
9 (10, 11, 12)" [23 (25.5, 28, 30.5) cm]

YARN

Medium-weight wool [4 MEDIUM]

Shown: Aussie Wool, 100% premium Australian wool, 128 yd. (118 m)/3.5 oz. (100 g): W10 Wild Fire, 5 (6, 6, 7) skeins

NEEDLES

Sizes 6 (4 mm) and 9 (5.5 mm) or sizes needed to obtain correct gauge

GAUGE

16 sts = 4" (10 cm) on size 9 needles in st pat

Take time to check gauge.

NOTIONS

Three stitch holders

Heavy-duty separating zipper, 22 (24, 24, 26)" [56 (61, 61, 66) cm]

Tapestry needle

Hand-sewing needle and thread

SIZES

Small (Medium, Large, X-Large)

Finished chest measurement: 44 (46, 48, 50)" [111.5 (116.5, 122, 127) cm]

Hefty Zippered Vest

For shoveling snow or toting firewood, a guy needs a sweater that will keep the chill off but free up his arms. This chunky wool vest is the answer. It has a zip front for quick-on-and-off, extra-deep armholes for layering over a heavy shirt, and roomy pockets to warm his hands.

The stitch pattern creates a highly textured rib design that traps air for extra warmth.

Patch pockets are knitted separately and sewn to the vest fronts.

BACK

With size 6 needles, CO 86 (90, 94, 98) sts.

Row 1 (RS): K2, *p2, k2, rep from * across row.

Row 2: P2, *k2, p2, rep from * across row.

Rep Rows 1 and 2 for 2½" (6.5 cm), ending with an RS row.

Change to size 9 needles. Work body pat as foll:

Row 1 (WS): P.

Row 2 (RS): K.

Row 3 (WS): P2, *k2, p2, rep from * across row.

Row 4 (RS): K2, *p2, k2, rep from * across row.

Rep Rows 1–4 until piece measures 13 (13½, 14, 14½)" [33 (34.5, 35.5, 37) cm] from beg, ending with a WS row.

Shape armholes: At beg of next 2 rows, BO 8 sts. Keeping pat as est, dec 1 st each side every row twice—66 (70, 74, 78) sts. Work even until armhole is 11 (11½, 12, 12½)" [28 (29, 30.5, 32) cm] from beg, ending with a WS row.

Shape shoulders: Work 16 (17, 18, 19) sts and place on holder to be joined later to right front, BO next 34 (36, 38, 40), work rem 16, (17, 18, 19) sts, and place on holder to be joined later to left front.

LEFT FRONT

With size 6 needles, CO 48 (49, 52, 53) sts.

Row 1 (RS): K2, *p2, k2, rep from * across row to last 2 (3, 2, 3) sts, place marker in work, k last 2 (3, 2, 3) sts.

Row 2: K2 (3, 2, 3), sl marker, p2, *k2, p2, rep from * across row.

Cont in this manner, working rib as for back and keeping 2 (3, 2, 3) sts at front edge in garter st for 2½" (6.5 cm).

Change to size 9 needles. Keeping 2 (3, 2, 3) sts in garter st, work same as back to armhole. Shape arm sides as for back, keeping front 2 (3, 2, 3) sts in garter st and working on 38 (39, 42, 43) sts until armhole is 8 (8½, 9, 10)" [20.5 (21.5, 23, 25.5) cm], ending at neck edge.

Shape neck: At beg of next row, BO 16 (17, 18, 19) sts. Cont in pat as established, dec 1 st at neck edge every other row 6 (5, 6, 5) times—16 (17, 18, 19) sts. Work even until armhole is 11 (11½, 12, 12½)" [28 (29, 30.5, 32) cm]. Do not BO. Place sts on holder to be joined later to back left shoulder.

RIGHT FRONT

With size 6 needles, CO 48 (49, 52, 53) sts.

Row 1 (RS): K2 (3, 2, 3), place marker, k2, *p2, k2, rep from * across row.

Row 2: P2, *k2, p2, rep from * to marker, sl marker, k2 (3, 2, 3).

Cont in this manner, working rib as for back and keeping 2 (3, 2, 3) sts at front edge in garter st for 2½" (6.5 cm).

Change to size 9 needles. Keeping 2 (3, 2, 3) sts in garter st, work same as back to armhole. Shape arm sides as for back, keeping front 2 (3, 2, 3) sts in garter st and working on 38 (39, 42, 43) sts until armhole is 8 (8½, 9, 10)" [20.5 (21.5, 23, 25.5) cm], ending at neck edge.

Shape neck: At beg of next row, BO 16 (17, 18, 19) sts. Cont in pat as established, dec 1 st at neck edge every other row 6 (5, 6, 5) times—16 (17, 18, 19) sts. Work until armhole is 11 (11½, 12, 12½)" [28 (29, 30.5, 32) cm]. Do not BO. Place sts on holder to be joined later to back right shoulder.

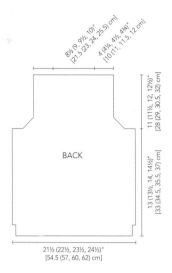

POCKETS

With size 9 needles, CO 26 (26, 30, 30) sts. Work pat as for back for 5" (12.5 cm), ending with a WS row. BO from RS in k. Repeat for second pocket.

COLLAR

With RS facing you, sl 16 (17, 18, 19) sts from right front and back shoulders from holders onto separate size 9 needles. Join using the 3-needle BO method. Join left front and back shoulders in the same manner.

With RS facing you, using size 6 needles, beg at top right front, pick up and k16 (17, 18, 19) sts along BO right front neck edge, k10 (9, 8, 7) sts along right front dec neck edge, k34 (36, 38, 40) sts along back of neck, k10 (9, 8, 7) sts along left front dec neck edge, then k16 (17, 18, 19) sts along BO left front neck edge—86 (88, 90, 92) sts.

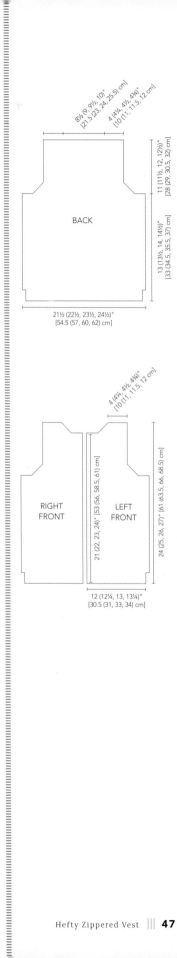

Row 1 (WS): K2 (3, 2, 3), place marker, p2, *k2, p2, rep from * to last 2 (3, 2, 3) sts, place marker, k last 2 (3, 2, 3) sts.

Row 2 (RS): K2 (3, 2, 3), sl marker, k2, *p2, k2, rep from * to next marker, sl marker, k2 (3, 2, 3).

Cont in this manner, working rib and keeping 2 (3, 2, 3) sts at front edge in garter st for 2" (5 cm). BO in rib.

ARMBANDS

With RS facing you, using size 6 needles, beg at underarm seam, pick up and k64 (66, 68, 70) sts along armhole edge to shoulder, then pick up and k64 (66, 68, 70) along other side of armhole—128 (132, 136, 140) sts. Work in k2, p2 rib for 3 rows. BO from RS in rib.

FINISHING

Sew underarm seams. Center pockets on fronts, just above border sts, then sew in place. Sew in zipper (see page 10). To preserve the texture, blocking is not recommended for this pattern.

YARN

Medium-weight wool/acrylic **4 MEDIUM**

Shown: Wool Ease by Lion Brand Yarn, 80% acrylic/20% wool, 3 oz. (85 g)/197 yd. (180 m): (A) #152 Oxford Grey, 5 (5, 6, 6) skeins; (B) #151 Grey Heather, 3 (3, 4, 4) skeins

NEEDLES

Sizes 5 (3.75) and 8 (5 mm) or sizes needed to obtain correct gauge

GAUGE

18 sts = 4" (10 cm) on size 8 needles in St st

Take time to check gauge.

NOTIONS

Sport zipper, 10" (25.5 cm)

Four stitch holders

SIZES

Small (Medium, Large, X-Large)

Finished chest measurement: 44 (46, 48, 50)" [111.5 (116.5, 122, 127) cm]

Alpine Zip-Neck Pullover

Choose two tones of his favorite color to knit this handsome sweater. Can't you just see him schussing down the slopes in this cozy, zip-neck pullover? The intricate-looking pattern at the top of the sleeves is really not hard to knit. The double-layer collar, front inset, and zipper require a little handwork, but the impressive results are well worth it.

This intricate stitch pattern at the top of the sleeves is worked in two colors. Make a practice swatch and you'll see that it's not as hard as it looks.

BACK

With size 5 needles and A, CO 100 (104, 108, 112) sts.

Bottom border:

Row 1: *K1, p1, rep from * across row.

Rep Row 1 until border is 2½" (6.5 cm).

Change to size 8 needles and work St st as foll:

Next row (RS): K across row.

Next row: P across row.

Rep last 2 rows until piece measures 15 (15½, 16, 16½)" [38 (39.5, 40.5, 42) cm] from beg, ending with a WS row.

Shape armholes: At beg of next 2 rows, BO 4 sts. Cont in pat as established on 92 (96, 100, 104) sts, until armhole measures 9 (9½, 10, 10½)" [23 (24, 25.5, 26.5) cm]. Do not BO; place all sts on a spare needle to be joined with front later.

FRONT

Work same as back until armhole measures 1 (1½, 2, 2½)" [2.5 (4, 5, 6.5) cm], ending with a p row.

Shape neck and zipper placket as foll:

Left front: Cont with A, k next 28 (30, 32, 34) sts, do not end off A, join B, k next 18 sts, place rem 46 (48, 50, 52) sts on holder to be worked later for right front. Work in St st as established, using both colors and always twisting colors as you change, taking the new color from under the color just worked until armhole measures 8 (8½, 9, 9½)" [20.5 (21.5, 23, 24) cm], ending with an RS row at neck edge.

Next row (WS): BO 18 B sts while purling, then work rem 28 (30, 32, 34) A sts. Working on these sts only, dec 1 st at neck edge every row 2 times. Work even on rem 26 (28, 30, 32) sts until piece measures same as back to shoulder. Place sts on holder to be joined later with back.

Right front: Place right front sts from holder onto needle, join a new ball of B at center neck edge, and k next 18 sts, do not end off B, join A, and k rem 28 (30, 32, 34) sts. Work even in pat as established until armhole measures 8 (8½, 9, 9½)" [20.5 (21.5, 23, 24) cm], ending with a WS row at neck edge.

Next row (RS): BO 18 B sts while knitting, end off B and k rem 28 (30, 32, 34) sts. Keep pat as established, dec 1 st at neck edge every row 2 times. Work even on rem 26 (28, 30, 32) sts until piece measures same as back to shoulder. Place sts on holder to be joined later with back.

SLEEVES

Make 2.

Sleeve border:

With size 5 needles and A, CO 48 (50, 52, 54) sts. Work border same as back, end with a WS row, end off A.

Change to size 8 needles and join B. K 1 row, inc 1 st at end of row—49 (51, 53, 55) sts. Cont in St st, inc 1 st each side every 4th row 16 (17, 18, 19) times—81 (85, 89, 93) sts.

Work even until sleeve measures 19½ (20, 20½, 21)" [49.5 (51, 52, 53.5) cm], ending with a k row.

Work sleeve pat as foll:

Row 1: With B, p across row.

Row 2: Join A, k1, *yarn back (yb), sl 1, yarn front (yf), sl 1, yb, sl 1, k1, rep from * across row.

Row 3: With A, p1, *yb, sl 3, wrap yarn around needle, p1, rep from * across row.

Row 4: With B, k across row, dropping extra wraps to make long loose strands in front of work.

Row 5: With B, p across row.

Row 6: With A, k1, *yb, sl 1, insert needle from the front under the loose strand and k the loose strand and the next st as one, yb, sl 1, k1, rep from * across row.

Row 7: With A, k1, *yf, sl 1, p1, yf, sl 1, k1, rep from * across row.

Row 8: With B, k across row.

Row 9: With B, p across row.

Row 10: With A, k1, *yf, sl 1, yb, k1, rep from * across row.

Rows 11–20: Rep Rows 1–10, reversing colors.

Row 21: With B, p across row.

BO in k.

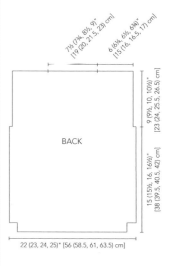

BACK

7½ (7¾, 8½, 9)" [19 (20, 21.5, 23) cm]

6 (6¼, 6½, 6¾)" [15 (16, 16.5, 17) cm]

9 (9½, 10, 10½)" [23 (24, 25.5, 26.5) cm]

15 (15½, 16, 16½)" [38 (39.5, 40.5, 42) cm]

22 (23, 24, 25)" [56 (58.5, 61, 63.5) cm]

FRONT

6 (6¼, 6½, 6¾)" [15 (16, 16.5, 17) cm]

8" [20.5 cm]

9 (9½, 10, 10½)" [23 (24, 25.5, 26.5) cm]

15 (15½, 16, 16½)" [38 (39.5, 40.5, 42) cm]

22 (23, 24, 25)" [56 (58.5, 61, 63.5) cm]

SLEEVE

18 (19, 20, 21)" [46 (48, 51, 53) cm]

21 (21½, 22, 22½)" [53 (54.4, 56, 57) cm]

9 (10, 11, 12)" [23 (25.5, 27.9, 30.5) cm]

COLLAR

Holding RS together, join 26 (28, 30, 32) sts of each shoulder together, using the 3-needle BO method. Leave center back 40 sts on holder to be worked for collar.

Using size 5 needles and B, with RS facing you, pick up 18 sts on BO front neck edge, 11 (12, 13, 14) sts along right neck shaping, k40 sts from back neck holder, pick up 11 (12, 13, 14) sts along left neck shaping, pick up 18 BO sts at top left—98 (100, 102, 104) sts. P 1 row. Cont in St st until collar is 3" (7.5 cm), ending with an RS row. K next row from the p side to form a turning ridge for collar. End off B, join A. K 1 row. Cont in St st until A is 2¾" (7 cm). BO.

FINISHING

Pin zipper in place from the turning ridge down to bottom of opening. Set in zipper following instructions on page 10.

When zipper is in place, fold collar to inside and sew sides to zipper back. Tack bottom of collar along neck edge.

Fold sleeve in half. Mark center of sleeve and pin to shoulder seam. Pin sleeve in place, then sew in sleeve. Sew underarm seams.

To block, place sweater on a bath towel, spritz with water, pat into shape, and allow to dry.

If your zipper is a little too long, here's an easy way to shorten it. Mark the zipper tape at the correct length. Using a needle and thread, stitch across the teeth several times at the mark, creating a new zipper stop. If your sewing machine has a wide enough zigzag stitch to clear the zipper teeth, you can do this by stitching in place with your machine. Be sure to knot the threads securely. Then simply cut the zipper off ½" (1.3 cm) below the stitches.

A turning ridge at the top of the two-tone, double-layer collar helps it lie flat.

YARN

Medium-weight
black acrylic/wool (A) **4 MEDIUM**

Shown: Décor by Patons,
75% acrylic/25% wool, 3.5 oz.
(100 g)/210 yd. (192 m): (A) #1603
Black, 4 (4, 4, 5) skeins

Medium-weight
self-striping wool/soy (B) **4 MEDIUM**

Shown: SWS by Patons, 70%
wool/30% soy, 2.8 oz. (80 g)/110 yd.
(100 m): (B) #70013 Natural Earth,
7 (8, 8, 9) skeins

NEEDLES

Sizes 5 (3.75 mm) and 9 (5.5 mm)
or sizes needed to obtain
correct gauge

GAUGE

18 sts = 4" (10 cm) on size 9
needles in pat

NOTIONS

Four stitch holders

Heavy-duty zipper, 24 (24, 26, 26)"
[61 (61, 66, 66) cm]

SIZES

Small (Medium, Large, X-Large)

Finished chest measurement:
44 (46, 48, 50)"
[111.5 (116.5, 122, 127) cm]

Multicolor Lattice Jacket

The unusual slip-stitch pattern used for this sweater-jacket creates a lattice network that appears to float over subtle stripes of color. The "background" yarn is a wool/soy self-striping yarn. You knit with both yarns at the same time, so the resulting floats on the wrong side add extra body and warmth.

The lattice stitch pattern is worked with both yarns at the same time. Knit a test swatch to check your gauge and become familiar with the pattern.

LATTICE STITCH PATTERN

Multiple of 6 sts plus 2, using colors A and B

Row 1 (RS): With B, with yarn in back (wyib) k1, sl 1, *k4, sl 2, rep from * to last 6 sts, k4, sl 1, k1.

Row 2: With B, with yarn in front (wyif) p1, sl 1, *p4, sl 2, rep from * to last 6 sts, k4, sl 1, p1.

Row 3: With A, rep Row 1.

Row 4: With A, k1, wyif sl 1, *wyib k4, wyif sl 2, rep from * to last 6 sts, k4, wyif sl 1, k1.

Row 5: With B, k3, *wyib sl 2, k4, rep from * to last 5 sts, sl 2, k3.

Row 6: With B, p3, *wyif sl 2, p4, rep from * to last 5 sts, sl 2, p3.

Row 7: With A, rep Row 5.

Row 8: With A, k3, *wyif sl 2, wyib k4, rep from * to last 5 sts, wyif sl 2, k3.

Rep Rows 1–8 for pat.

Note: Be careful not to draw the yarn too tightly across the back of work when slipping stitches.

BACK

With size 5 needles and A, CO 98 (104, 110, 116) sts. K1, p1 in rib for 2½" (6.5 cm).

Change to size 9 needles. K 2 rows, do not end off A, join B, carry both colors up along sides as you work pat.

Cont with size 9 needles, rep 8 pat rows until piece measures 15 (15½, 16, 16½)" [38 (39.5, 40.5, 42) cm] from beg, ending with a WS row.

Shape armholes: At beg of next 2 rows, BO 6 sts. Being sure to keep pat as established, work even on rem 86 (92, 98, 104) sts until armhole measures 7 (7½, 8, 8½)" [18 (19, 20.5, 21.5) cm]. End off B.

Change to size 5 needles. Cont with A in garter st (k every row) for yoke until armhole measures 9 (9½, 10, 10½)" [23 (24, 25.5, 26.5) cm], ending with a WS row.

Shape shoulders: K across 26 (28, 30, 32) sts for right shoulder and place these sts on holder to be joined to front later, BO center 34 (36, 38, 40) sts for back neck, place rem 26 (28, 30, 32) sts on holder for left shoulder.

LEFT FRONT

With size 5 needles and A, CO 51 (51, 57, 63) sts.

Row 1: K1 *p1, k1, rep from * across row.

Row 2: P1 *k1, p1, rep from * across row.

Rep Rows 1 and 2 until border is 2½" (6.5 cm), dec 1 st at end of last row—50 (50, 56, 62) sts.

Change to size 9 needles. K 2 rows, do not end off A, join B, carry both colors up along sides as you work pat. Work pat same as back to armhole, ending with a WS row.

Shape armhole: At beg of next row, BO 6 sts. Being sure to keep pat as established, work even on 44 (44, 50, 56) sts until armhole measures 7 (7½, 8, 8½)" [18 (19, 20.5, 21.5) cm], ending with a WS row. End off B.

Change to size 5 needles and cont with A.

Shape yoke and neck: K 1 row.

Next row: K, BO 12 (12, 14, 16) sts, k to end of row.

Cont in garter st, dec 1 st at neck edge every row 6 (4, 6, 8) times.

Work even in garter st until yoke is same as back. Place rem 26 (28, 30, 32) sts on holder to be joined to back later.

RIGHT FRONT

Work same as left front to armhole, ending with an RS row.

Shape armhole: At beg of next row, BO 6 sts. Being sure to keep pat as established, work even on 44 (44, 50, 56) sts until armhole measures 7 (7½, 8, 8½)" [18 (19, 20.5, 21.5) cm], ending with a WS row. End off B.

Change to size 5 needles and cont with A.

Shape yoke and neck: At beg of next row, BO 12 (12, 14, 16) sts, k to end of row.

Cont in garter st, dec 1 st at neck edge every row 6 (4, 6, 8) times. Work even in garter st until yoke is same as back. Place rem 26 (28, 30, 32) sts on holder to be joined to back later.

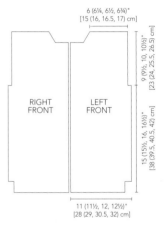

SLEEVES

Make 2.

With size 5 needles and A, CO 46 (48, 50, 52) sts. K1, p1 in rib for 2½" (6.5 cm). K 1 row, inc 4 (2, 6, 4) sts evenly spaced across row—50 (50, 56, 56) sts.

Change to size 9 needles. K across row. Join A, work pat same as back; AT THE SAME TIME, inc 1 st each side every 8th row (being sure to form new pats as sts are increased) 15 (16, 17, 18) times—80 (82, 90, 92) sts. Work even until sleeve measures 19 (19½, 20, 20½)" [48.5 (49.5, 51, 52) cm] from beg, ending with a WS row. End off B.

Change to size 5 needles. Continue with A in garter st until sleeve measures 21 (21½, 22, 22½)" [53.5 (54.5, 56, 57) cm] from beg, ending with a WS row. BO loosely.

NECKBAND

With RS facing, sl sts from right front and back shoulders from holders onto size 5 needles. Join using three-needle BO method. Join left front and back shoulders in the same manner.

Using size 5 needles and A, with RS facing you, pick up 12 (12, 14, 16) sts along BO right front, pick up 13 sts along right front shaped edge, pick up 34 (36, 38, 40) sts along BO back neck, pick up 14 sts along left front shaped edge, then pick up 12 (12, 14, 16) sts along BO left front—85 (87, 93, 99) sts.

Row 1: K1, *p1, k1, rep from * across row.

Row 2: P1, *k1, p1, rep from * across row.

Rep Rows 1 and 2 until neckband is 3" (7.5 cm). BO in rib pat.

RIGHT FRONT BAND

Using size 5 needles and A, with RS facing you, starting at bottom right corner, pick up 10 sts along edge of bottom border, 100 (104, 108, 112) sts along right front until neckband, then pick up 14 sts along edge of neckband—124 (128, 132, 136) sts. K 1 row. BO in k.

LEFT FRONT BAND

Using size 5 needles and A, with RS facing you, starting at top right corner, pick up 14 sts along edge of neckband, 100 (104, 108, 112) sts along left front until bottom border, then pick up 10 sts along edge of bottom border—124, (128, 132, 136) sts. K 1 row. BO in k.

FINISHING

Fold sleeve in half. Mark center of sleeve and pin to shoulder seam. Pin sleeve in place, then sew in sleeve. Sew underarm seams. Sew in zipper (see page 10).

Blocking is not recommended for this garment to preserve the texture of the pattern.

Rows of black garter stitch top off the front and back. When joined together, they create a yoke at the shoulder.

YARN

Lightweight yarn **3 LIGHT**

Shown: Pure by South West Trading Company, 100% Soy Silk, 1.76 oz. (50 g)/164 yd. (150 m): #027 Cabernet, 7 (8, 8, 9) balls

NEEDLES

Sizes 3 (3.25 mm) and 6 (4 mm) or sizes needed to obtain correct gauge

Size 3 (3.25 mm) circular needle, 24" (61 cm) long

GAUGE

26 sts = 4" (10 cm) on size 6 needles in cable pat

NOTIONS

Four stitch holders

Two stitch markers

Tapestry needle

SIZES

Small (Medium, Large, X-Large)

Finished chest measurement: 44 (46, 48, 50)" [111.5 (116.5, 122, 127) cm]

Cabled V-Neck Vest

For the look and touch of pure luxury, knit him this fine-gauge cabled vest. It can be worn casually with slacks or jeans, but it's also great layered under a sport coat or suit jacket. This is an easy cable to knit, even if cables are new to you, and you'll love the feeling of this soy silk yarn slipping through your fingers.

Small, neat claw cables are set off by reverse stockinette stitch and separated by garter-stitch bands.

A generous ribbing band at the bottom is knitted on smaller needles for a snugger fit.

BACK

With size 3 straight needles, CO 142 (148, 154, 160) sts. K1, p1 in rib for 2½" (6.5 cm), inc 1 st at end of last row—143 (149, 155, 161) sts.

Change to size 6 needles and work cable pat as follows:

Row 1 (RS): K5 (8, 11, 14), *k10, p2, k8, p2, rep from * twice, k1 (center st), **p2, k8, p2, k10, rep from ** twice, end with k5 (8, 11, 14).

Row 2: K5 (8, 11, 14), *p1, k8, p1, k2, p8, k2, rep from * twice, p1 (center st), **k2, p8, k2, p1, k8, p1, rep from ** twice, end k5 (8, 11, 14).

Row 3: Rep Row 1.

Row 4: Rep Row 2.

Row 5 (cable twist row): K5 (8, 11, 14), *k10, p2, sl next 2 sts to cable needle and hold to back of work, k next 2 sts, k2 from cable needle, sl next 2 sts to cable needle, hold to front of work, k next 2 sts, k2 from cable needle (cable twist made), p2, rep from * twice, k1 (center st), **p2, cable twist on next 8 sts, p2, k10, rep from ** twice, ending k5 (8, 11, 14).

Rep Rows 2–5 until back is 13½ (14, 14½, 15)" [34.5 (35.5, 37, 38) cm] from beg, ending with a WS row.

Shape armholes: At beg of next 2 rows, BO 6 (7, 8, 9) sts—131 (135, 139, 143) sts. Being sure to keep pat as established, dec 1 st each arm side every other row 7 times—117 (121, 125,129) sts.

Being sure to keep pat as established, work even until armhole is 10½ (11, 11½, 12)" [26.5 (28, 29, 30.5) cm].

Shape shoulders: Work across 39 (40, 41, 42) sts and place on holder to be joined later to front right shoulder, BO center 39 (41, 43, 45) sts, work across rem 39 (40, 41, 42) sts and place on holder to be joined later to front left front shoulder.

FRONT

Work same as back until armhole shaping is completed, ending with a WS row.

Divide for V-neck:

Left front: Work across 58 (60, 62, 64) sts, place rem 59 (61, 63, 65) sts on holder to be worked later for right front, turn. Work 1 row even. Cont in pat, dec 1 st at neck edge on next row, then every other row twice more, then every 4th row 16 (17, 18, 19) times—39 (40, 41, 42) sts. Work even until armhole is same length as back to shoulder. Place rem sts on holder to be joined later to left back shoulder.

Right front: Place center st on a pin to be worked later for V-shaping, join yarn at center, and work rem 58 (60, 62, 64) sts, turn. Work 1 row even. Dec 1 st at neck edge on next row, then every other row twice more, then every 4th row 16 (17, 18, 19) times—39 (40, 41, 42) sts. Work even until armhole is same length as back to shoulder. Do not BO; leave sts on holder to be joined later to back right shoulder.

FINISHING

With RS together, sl sts from right front and back shoulders onto size 6 needles. Join using the three-needle BO method. Join left front and back shoulders in the same manner.

Sew underarm seams.

V-NECK BORDER

Using size 3 circular needle, with RS facing you, starting at right side of back, pick up 40 (42, 44, 46) sts along back neck (note: when back of neck was BO there were only 39 [41, 43, 45] sts, but an even number is needed to make V-shaping), pick up 56 (58, 60, 62) sts along left side of V, place marker, k center st from pin, place marker, pick up 56 (58, 60, 62) sts along right side of V, mark this as end of row.

Row 1: *K1, p1, rep from * until 2 sts before the first marker, sl 1, k1, psso, sl marker, k center st, sl marker, k2tog, **p1, k1, rep from ** to end.

Row 2: Follow rib to center st, k center st, follow rib to end of row.

Row 3: Rep Row 1.

Row 4: Rep Row 2.

BO in rib, following Row 1 decs at center as you BO.

ARMBANDS

Using size 3 circular needle, with RS facing you, starting at underarm seam, pick up 76 (78, 80, 82) sts to shoulder seam, then pick up 76 (78, 80, 82) sts from shoulder to armhole seam—152 (156, 160, 164) sts.

Rows 1–4: *K 1, p 1, rep from * across row.

BO in rib.

Blocking is not recommended for this garment to preserve the texture of the stitch pattern.

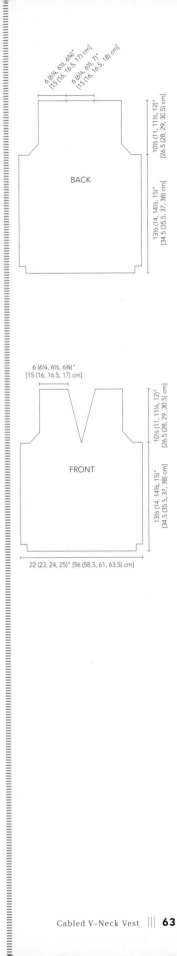

YARN

Medium-weight wool

Shown: Torino by Tahki Stacy Charles, 100% merino wool, 1.75 oz. (50 g)/94 yd. (85 m): #105 gold, 18 (18, 19, 20) balls

NEEDLES

Sizes 4 (3.5 mm) and 8 (5 mm) or sizes needed to obtain correct gauge

GAUGE

18 sts = 4" (10 cm) on size 8 needles in pat

NOTIONS

Four stitch holders

Four buttons, ¾" (2 cm) diameter

Tapestry needle

SIZES

Small (Medium, Large, X-Large)

Finished chest measurement: 44 (46, 48, 50)" [111.5 (116.5, 122, 127) cm]

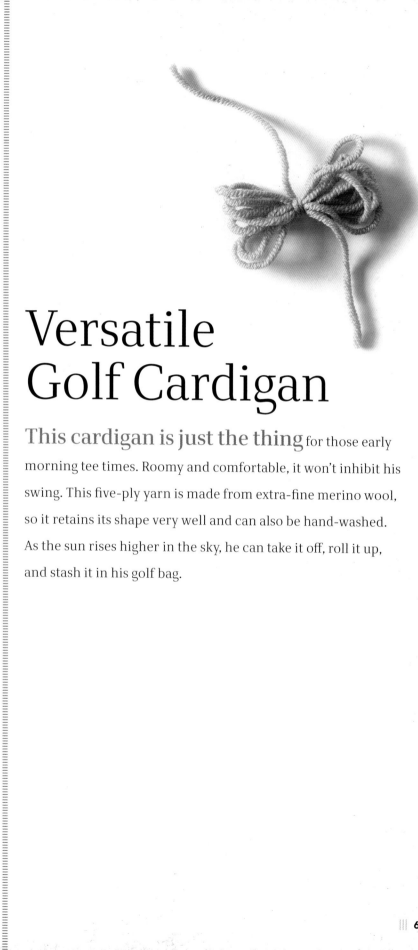

Versatile Golf Cardigan

This cardigan is just the thing for those early morning tee times. Roomy and comfortable, it won't inhibit his swing. This five-ply yarn is made from extra-fine merino wool, so it retains its shape very well and can also be hand-washed. As the sun rises higher in the sky, he can take it off, roll it up, and stash it in his golf bag.

This easy pattern of knit and purl stitches repeats every 16 rows to create a dynamic diagonal design.

BACK

With size 4 needles, CO 100 (104, 108, 112) sts. K1, p1 in rib for 2½" (6.5 cm).

Change to size 8 needles and work pat as foll:

Row 1 and all odd-numbered rows (RS): K across row.

Row 2: P2 (0, 2, 0), *k4, p4, rep from * across row, end p2 (0, 2, 0).

Row 4: Rep Row 2.

Row 6: K4 (2, 4, 2), *p 4, k 4, rep from * across row, end last rep k4 (2, 4, 2).

Row 8: Rep Row 6.

Row 10: K2 (0, 2, 0), *p4, k 4, rep from * across row, end k2 (0, 2, 0).

Row 12: Rep Row 10.

Row 14: P4 (2, 4, 2), *k4, p4, rep from * across row, end last rep p4 (2, 4, 2).

Row 16: Rep Row 14.

Rep Rows 1–16 for pat until back measures 15 (15½, 16, 16½)" [38 (39.5, 40.5, 42) cm] from beg, ending with a WS row.

Shape armholes: At beg of next 2 rows, BO 8 sts. Being sure to keep pat as established, work rem 84 (88, 92, 96) sts until armhole is 9 (9½, 10, 10½)" [23 (24, 25.5, 26.5) cm], ending with a WS row.

Shape shoulders: Work across 26 (27, 27, 28) sts and place on holder to be joined to front right shoulder, BO center 32 (34, 38, 40) sts for back neck, work rem 26 (27, 27, 28) sts and place on holder to be joined to front left shoulder.

▌RIGHT FRONT

With size 4 needles, CO 56 (60, 64, 68) sts.

Bottom border:

Row 1 (RS): K8, place marker, *p1, k1, rep from * across row.

Row 2: *P1, k1, rep from * to marker, sl marker, p1, k7.

Rep Rows 1 and 2 until border is 2½" (6.5 cm), ending with a WS row.

Change to size 8 needles and keeping the 8 sts at front edge in pat as established, work textured pat on rem 48 (52, 56, 60) as foll:

Row 1 and all odd-numbered rows (RS): K.

Row 2: P0 (2, 0, 2), *k4, p4, rep from * across row, end p0 (2, 0, 2).

Row 4: Rep Row 2.

Row 6: K2 (4, 2, 4), *p4, k4, rep from * across row, end last rep k2 (4, 2, 4).

Row 8: Rep Row 6.

Row 10: K0 (2, 0, 2), *p4, k4, rep from * across row, end k0 (2, 0, 2).

Row 12: Rep Row 10.

Row 14: P2 (4, 2, 4), *k4, p4, rep from * across row, end last rep p2 (4, 2, 4).

Row 16: Rep Row 14.

Rep Rows 1–16 until front is 8" (20.5 cm) from beg.

Shape V-neck: Cont in pat as established, dec 1 st at front edge, making dec on the 2 sts inside front border, rep the dec every 6th row twice, then every 4th row; AT THE SAME TIME, when front is same as back to armhole, BO 8 sts at arm side. Cont following pat as established, making front edge decs every 4th row until 34 (35, 35, 36) sts rem Work even until armhole is 9 (9½, 10, 10½)" [23 (24, 25.5, 26.5) cm], ending with a WS row.

Next row: Work 8 border sts, place rem 26 (27, 27, 28) sts on holder to be joined to right back shoulder. Cont on 8 border sts for 2 (2½, 2½, 3)" [5 (6.5, 6.5, 7.5) cm]. BO.

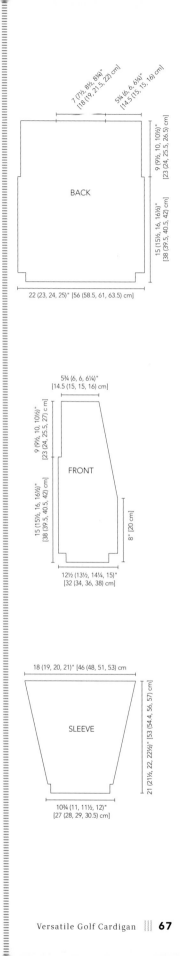

BACK

7 (7½, 8½, 8¾)"
[18 (19, 21.5, 22) cm]

5¾ (6, 6, 6¼)"
[14.5 (15, 15, 16) cm]

9 (9½, 10, 10½)"
[23 (24, 25.5, 26.5) cm]

15 (15½, 16, 16½)"
[38 (39.5, 40.5, 42) cm]

22 (23, 24, 25)" [56 (58.5, 61, 63.5) cm]

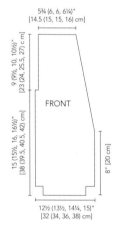

5¾ (6, 6, 6¼)"
[14.5 (15, 15, 16) cm]

FRONT

9 (9½, 10, 10½)"
[23 (24, 25.5, 27) c m]

15 (15½, 16, 16½)"
[38 (39.5, 40.5, 42) cm]

8" [20 cm]

12½ (13½, 14¼, 15)"
[32 (34, 36, 38) cm]

18 (19, 20, 21)" [46 (48, 51, 53) cm]

SLEEVE

21 (21½, 22, 22½)" [53 (54.4, 56, 57) cm]

10¾ (11, 11½, 12)"
[27 (28, 29, 30.5) cm]

LEFT FRONT

With size 4 needles, CO 56 (60, 64, 68) sts.

Bottom border:

Row 1 (RS): *K1, p1, rep from * to last 8 sts, place marker, k8.

Row 2: K7, p1, sl marker, *k1, p1, rep from * to end.

Rep Rows 1 and 2 for pat, making first buttonhole ½" (1.3 cm) from bottom, then 3 more buttonholes 2½" (6.5 cm) apart. To make buttonholes, on 8 border sts of front edge, on a RS row, k4, yo, k2tog, k2. On next WS row: K7, p1.

Work border for 2½" (6.5 cm).

Change to size 8 needles and work pat same as right front, reversing all V-neck and armhole shaping.

SLEEVES

Make 2.

With size 4 needles, CO 44 (48, 52, 56) sts. K1, p1 in rib for 2½" (6.5 cm).

Next row: K, inc 4 sts evenly across row—48 (52, 56, 60) sts.

Change to size 8 needles. P 1 row, then beg textured pat as for back on center 48 (48, 56, 56) sts and work for 1" (2.5 cm), inc 1 st each side. Being sure to form new pats as sts are inc, rep inc each side every 6th row 6 times more—62 (66, 70, 74) sts. Then cont inc 1 st each side every 8th row 10 times—82 (86, 90, 94) sts. Work even in pat until sleeve is 21 (21½, 22, 22½)" [53.5 (54.5, 56, 57) cm] from beg. BO.

FINISHING

With RS together, using three-needle BO method, join right and left front shoulders to back. Sew neck tabs together, centered on back neck. Sew in place.

Fold sleeve in half. Mark center of sleeve and pin to shoulder seam. Pin sleeve in place, then sew in sleeve. Sew underarm seams. Sew on buttons.

Blocking is not recommended to preserve the texture of the garment.

| TIP

When you sew on buttons, be sure to pass the thread over a couple stitches to prevent the button from pulling too much. Insert a knitting needle or cable needle under the button between the holes to create a "shank" as you sew the button on. This will make room for the thickness of the buttonhole band.

A deep V neckline with a garter-stitch border comes together with a four-button closure.

YARN

Fine wool

Shown: Gems by Louet North America, 100% merino wool, 3.5 oz. (100 g)/225 yd. (207 m): (MC) #39 Fern, 4 skeins; (A) #44 Sandalwood, 2 skeins; (B) #47 Terra Cotta, ½ skein (available in 50 g ball)

NEEDLES

Sizes 3 (3.25 mm) and 5 (3.75 mm) or sizes needed to obtain correct gauge

Size 3 (3.25 mm) circular needle, 24" (61 cm) long

GAUGE

24 sts = 4" (10 cm) on size 5 needles in St st

Take time to check gauge.

NOTIONS

Five stitch holders

Tapestry needle

SIZES

Small (Medium, Large, X-Large)

Finished chest measurement: 44 (46, 48, 50)" [111.5 (116.5, 122, 127) cm]

Color Block Pullover

For the guy who likes something out of the ordinary, here's a color-blocked pullover with an interesting intarsia pattern across the chest and at the sleeve tops. The rolled neckline gives it another unusual twist. Made from sport-weight merino wool, this sweater is also soft and comfortable to wear.

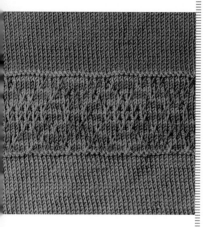

Choose contrasting colors to make this intarsia pattern more apparent.

YOKE INTARSIA PATTERN

Note: On all RS rows, sl all sl sts with yarn in back.

Row 1 (RS): With A, k3, *(sl 1, k8) twice, sl 1, k3, rep from * across row.

Row 2 and all WS rows: Knit or purl the sts worked on previous row, with the same color; sl all the sl sts with yarn in front of work.

Row 3: With B, k4, *(sl 1, k1) 3 times, k6, (sl 1, k1) 3 times, k4, rep from *, end last rep k3.

Row 5: With A, k9, *sl 1, k5, sl 1, k15, rep from *, end last rep k9 instead of k15.

Row 7: With B (k1, sl 1) 3 times, *k4, sl 1, k3, sl 1, k4, (sl 1, k1) 4 times, sl 1, rep from *, end with k4, sl 1, k3, sl, 1, k4, (sl 1, k1) 3 times.

Row 9: With A, k6, *sl 1, k4, sl 1, k1, sl 1, k4, sl 1, k9, rep from *, end last rep k6 instead of k9.

Row 11: With B, k2, sl 1, k4, sl 1, k9, sl 1, k4, sl 1, k1, rep from *, end k1 after last rep.

Row 13: With A, k3, *sl 1, k4, (sl 1, k1) 4 times, sl 1, k4, sl 1, k3, rep from * across row.

Row 15: With B, k4, *sl 1, k15, sl 1, k5, rep from *, end last rep k4 instead of k5.

Rows 17 and 18: With A, rep Rows 13 and 14.

Rows 19 and 20: With B, rep Rows 11 and 12.

Rows 21 and 22: With A rep Rows 9 and 10.

Rows 23 and 24: With B rep Rows 7 and 8.

Row 25 and 26: With A, rep Rows 5 and 6.

Rows 27 and 28: With B rep Rows 2 and 3.

BACK

With size 3 needles and MC, CO 132 (138, 144, 150) sts.

K1, p1 rib for 2½" (6.5 cm).

Change to size 5 needles and work as foll:

Row 1 (RS): K.

Row 2: P.

Rep Rows 1 and 2 until back is 15 (15½, 16, 16½)" [38 (39.5, 40.5, 42) cm] from beg, ending with a WS row.

Shape armholes: At beg of next 2 rows, BO 6 (6, 6, 6) sts—120 (126, 132, 138) sts. End off MC.

Join B, k 1 row.

Next row: With B, k, inc 1 (1, 3, 1) sts evenly spaced across row—121 (127, 135, 139) sts. Do not end off B but carry up sides as you work pat.

Join A, beg Yoke Pat:

Row 1: K4 (7, 0, 2), place marker, work Row 1 of Yoke Intarsia Pat until last 4 (7, 0, 2) sts, place marker, k last 4 (7, 0, 2).

Row 2: K4 (7, 0, 2), sl marker, work Row 2 of Yoke Intarsia Pat until last 4 (7, 0, 2) sts, sl marker, k last 4 (7, 0, 2).

Cont to work in this manner, following Yoke Intarsia Pat and keeping 4 (7, 0, 2) sts each side in garter st (k every row) until 28 pat rows are worked.

Knit 2 rows in B, end off B. Cont in A, working in St st until armhole measures 9 (9½, 10, 10½)" [23 (24, 25.5, 26.5) cm].

Shape shoulders: Work 40 (41, 42, 43) sts, place these sts on holder to be joined later to front right shoulder, work next 41 (45, 51, 53) sts and place on holder to be worked later for back neck, work rem 40 (41, 42, 43) sts and place on holder to be joined later to front left shoulder.

┃ FRONT

Work same as back until armhole measures 6 (6½, 7, 7½)" [15 (16.5, 18, 19) cm].

Shape neck:

Left front: Work 45 (46, 47, 48) sts for left front, place next 31 (35, 41, 43) sts on holder for center front neck, place next 45 (46, 47, 48) sts on another holder for right front. Working on left front sts only, dec 1 st at neck edge every k row 5 (5, 5, 5) times—40 (41, 42, 43) sts. Work even until same as back to shoulder, place sts on holder to be joined later to back.

Right front: Sl right front sts from holder onto needle, join a new ball of yarn at neck edge, and k these sts. Cont in St st, dec 1 st at neck edge every k row 5 (5, 5, 5) times. Work even on rem 40 (41, 42, 43) sts until same length as back to shoulder. Place sts on holder to be joined later to back.

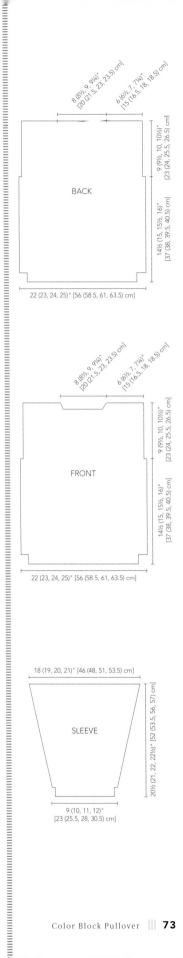

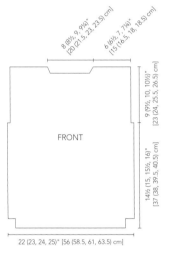

8 (8½, 9, 9¼)"
[20 (21.5, 23, 23.5) cm]

6 (6½, 7, 7¼)"
[15 (16.5, 18, 18.5) cm]

9 (9½, 10, 10½)"
[23 (24, 25.5, 26.5) cm]

BACK

14½ (15, 15½, 16)"
[37 (38, 39.5, 40.5) cm]

22 (23, 24, 25)" [56 (58.5, 61, 63.5) cm]

8 (8½, 9, 9¼)"
[20 (21.5, 23, 23.5) cm]

6 (6½, 7, 7¼)"
[15 (16.5, 18, 18.5) cm]

9 (9½, 10, 10½)"
[23 (24, 25.5, 26.5) cm]

FRONT

14½ (15, 15½, 16)"
[37 (38, 39.5, 40.5) cm]

22 (23, 24, 25)" [56 (58.5, 61, 63.5) cm]

18 (19, 20, 21)" [46 (48, 51, 53.5) cm]

SLEEVE

20½ (21, 22, 22½)" [52 (53.5, 56, 57) cm]

9 (10, 11, 12)"
[23 (25.5, 28, 30.5) cm]

SLEEVES

Make 2.

With size 3 needles and MC, CO 56 (60, 64, 68) sts. K1, p1 in rib for 2½" (6.5 cm). K next row, inc 11 sts evenly spaced across row—67 (71, 75, 79) sts. P 1 row.

Change to size 5 needles. Work in St st, inc 1 st each side every 5th row 21 (22, 23, 24) times—109 (115, 121, 127) sts. Work even until sleeve measures 17½ (18, 18½, 19)" [44.5 (45.5, 47, 48.5) cm] from beg, ending with a WS row. End off MC. Join B. K 2 rows, do not end off B. Join A.

Work Yoke Pat as foll:

Row 1: K9 (1, 4, 7), place marker, work Row 1 of Yoke Intarsia Pat until last 9 (1, 4, 7) sts, place marker, k last 9 (1, 4, 7) sts.

Row 2: K9 (1, 4, 7), sl marker, work Row 2 of Yoke Intarsia Pat until last 9 (1, 4, 7) sts, sl marker, k last 9 (1, 4, 7) sts.

Cont to work in this manner, following yoke pat, and keeping 9 (1, 4, 7) sts each side in garter st (k every row), until 28 pattern rows are worked.

K 2 rows in B. End off B. Cont in A, working in St st for 2 rows. BO.

NECKBAND

Holding RS together, join 40 (41, 42, 43) sts of each shoulder together, using the three-needle BO method.

Using size 3 circular needle and MC, with RS facing you and starting at right shoulder, k41 (45, 51, 53) sts from back neck holder, pick up 22 (24, 26, 28) sts along left front shaping, k31 (35, 41, 43) sts from center front holder, pick up 22 (24, 26, 28) sts along right front shaping—116 (128, 144, 152) sts. Mark here for end of row. Join and work around in St st (k every round) for 10 rounds. BO.

FINISHING

Fold sleeve in half. Mark center of sleeve and pin to shoulder seam. Pin sleeve in place, then sew in sleeve. Sew underarm seams.

To block garment, place on a towel, spritz with water, pat into shape, cover with a second towel, and allow to dry thoroughly.

If you like this sweater but you're not crazy about the rolled neck, simple work the neck stitches in ribbing, following the directions for one of the other crew neck sweaters. Another alternative is to work a few rows of stockinette, then a turning row, and a few more rows of stockinette to make a faced neckline, similar to the collar of the Alpine Zip-Neck Sweater.

Ten rows of stockinette stitch knitted on a small circular needle make the neckline roll to the outside.

YARN

Medium-weight (A)

Shown: Inca Alpaca by Classic Elite, 100% alpaca, 1.75 oz. (50 g)/109 yd. (100 m): (A) #1107 Camacho Periwinkle, 7 (7, 8, 8) skeins

Medium-weight (B)

Shown: Inca Print by Classic Elite, 100% alpaca, 1.75 oz. (50 g)/109 yd. (100 m): (B) #4648 Topiary, 10 (10, 11, 11) skeins

NEEDLES

For Small and Medium:

Sizes 4 (3.5 mm), 6 (4 mm), and 7 (4.5 mm) straight needles; size 4 (3.5 mm) circular needle, 24" (61 cm) long

For Large and X-Large:

Sizes 5 (3.75 mm) and 7 (4.5 mm) straight needles; size 5 (3.75 mm) circular needle, 24" (61 cm) long

or sizes needed to obtain correct gauge

GAUGE

For Small or Medium:

22 sts = 4" (10 cm) on size 6 needles in pat

For Large or X-Large:

20 sts = 4" (10 cm) on size 7 needles in pat

Take time to check gauge.

NOTIONS

Six stitch holders

SIZES

Small/Medium (Large/X-Large)

Finished chest measurement: 46 (50)" [116.5 (127) cm]

Entrelac Pullover

The entrelac stitch pattern is one of the most unusual. It does take some concentration, but the results are well worth it. Here I've combined a print yarn with a heather yarn to add even more richness to the design.

Notes:

1 The finished chest sizes are the same for Small and Medium and the same for Large and X-Large; the bottom borders and lengths are different.

2 Entrelac is a series of little rectangles and half rectangles (called triangles from now on) of knitting attached to each other both by picking up stitches and by knitting stitches together with ones from the previous tier. Every other tier is comprised of 9 full rectangles. The alternate rows are 1 triangle on each side and 8 full rectangles in the center. Each triangle or rectangle is 20 rows; when all the triangles are finished, it almost looks like the tiers of blocks are woven.

3 The technique used in this pattern is short rowing. When the directions say, "Turn," turn your work around completely and head back the way you came. Each tier is made up of rectangles (or triangles) and each of these is worked on 10 stitches, using the short row method to create each section. You will notice psso or p2tog at the end of many of the rows. This is where you are attaching the side of the rectangle that you are making to the top of the rectangle (or triangle) from the tier below.

4 A helpful hint is to try not to stop in the middle of a tier. If you must stop, make a note of which direction you were going in before you stopped.

BACK

With size 4 (4, 5, 5) straight needles and A, CO 114 (116, 120, 124) sts.

K1, p1 in rib for 2" (5 cm). K 1 row, dec 24 (26, 30, 34) sts evenly spaced across row—90 (90, 90, 90) sts. P 1 row. End off A, join B.

Change to size 6 (6, 7, 7) needles and work entrelac pat as follows:

Base Tier (RS):

First triangle: *K2, turn, p2, turn, k3, turn, p3, turn, k4, turn, p4, turn, k5, turn, p5, turn, k6, turn, p6, turn, k7, turn, p7, turn, k8, turn, p8, turn, k9, turn, p9, turn, k10, do not turn (first half rectangle completed). Rep from * 8 times more (9 triangles in all). Turn work to WS.

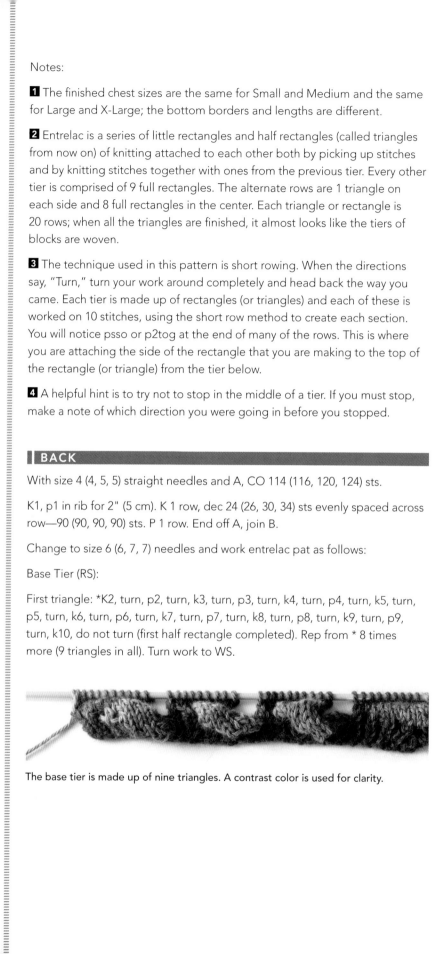

The base tier is made up of nine triangles. A contrast color is used for clarity.

Tier 2 (WS):

Step A: First triangle: Begin by purling and knitting into the first st (inc made), p2tog, turn the work and k3, p and k into the first st (inc made), p1, p2tog, turn, k4. Cont in this manner, inc 1 st in the first st and having 1 more p st between the p2tog, until there are 10 sts on right hand needle. Do not turn after the last p2tog.

Step B: Full rectangle: Leaving the 10 sts on the right hand needle, begin to work a full rectangle on the WS. Insert the needle from back to front, pick up and p 10 sts along the side edge of the first triangle from the tier below. Sl the last st picked up back to the left hand needle and p it together with the first st of the second triangle, turn, *k10, turn, p9, p2tog (1 st from the next triangle), rep from * until all 10 sts from the triangle have been worked. The rectangle is now complete and joined to the second side of the triangle.

Rep Step B until all the rectangles are formed across row. (You will have 1 triangle at beg, and 8 rectangles.)

Step C: Last triangle: Pick up and p9 from the unworked side of last triangle, turn, k9, turn, p7, p2tog, turn, k8. Cont with p2tog at the end of every WS row until 1 st rem, turn. (You will have 8 rectangles, and 1 triangle each side.)

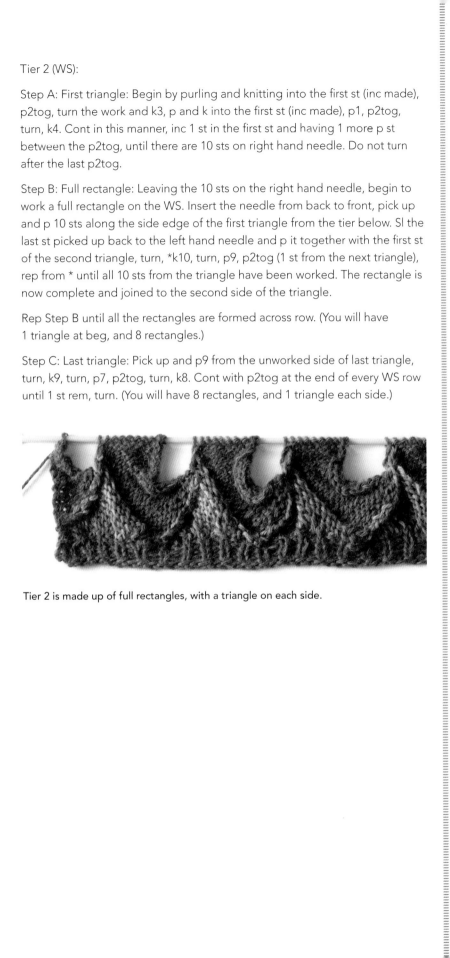

Tier 2 is made up of full rectangles, with a triangle on each side.

Tier 3 (RS):

Step A: Counting the 1 st left on the right hand needle, pick up and k9 along the first triangle, k the first st from the full rectangle and sl the last picked up st over it.

Step B: *Turn, p10, turn, k9, sl 1 st, knit 1 st from the rectangle and psso. Rep the last 2 rows until all 10 sts from the rectangle have been worked and are on the right hand needle, then pick up and k10 along the side edge of the next rectangle.

Rep Step B until 9 rectangles are completed.

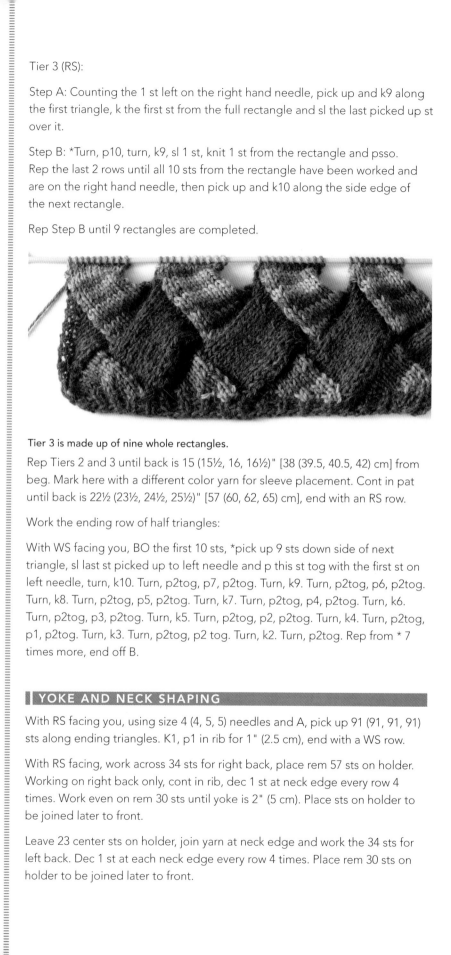

Tier 3 is made up of nine whole rectangles.

Rep Tiers 2 and 3 until back is 15 (15½, 16, 16½)" [38 (39.5, 40.5, 42) cm] from beg. Mark here with a different color yarn for sleeve placement. Cont in pat until back is 22½ (23½, 24½, 25½)" [57 (60, 62, 65) cm], end with an RS row.

Work the ending row of half triangles:

With WS facing you, BO the first 10 sts, *pick up 9 sts down side of next triangle, sl last st picked up to left needle and p this st tog with the first st on left needle, turn, k10. Turn, p2tog, p7, p2tog. Turn, k9. Turn, p2tog, p6, p2tog. Turn, k8. Turn, p2tog, p5, p2tog. Turn, k7. Turn, p2tog, p4, p2tog. Turn, k6. Turn, p2tog, p3, p2tog. Turn, k5. Turn, p2tog, p2, p2tog. Turn, k4. Turn, p2tog, p1, p2tog. Turn, k3. Turn, p2tog, p2 tog. Turn, k2. Turn, p2tog. Rep from * 7 times more, end off B.

YOKE AND NECK SHAPING

With RS facing you, using size 4 (4, 5, 5) needles and A, pick up 91 (91, 91, 91) sts along ending triangles. K1, p1 in rib for 1" (2.5 cm), end with a WS row.

With RS facing, work across 34 sts for right back, place rem 57 sts on holder. Working on right back only, cont in rib, dec 1 st at neck edge every row 4 times. Work even on rem 30 sts until yoke is 2" (5 cm). Place sts on holder to be joined later to front.

Leave 23 center sts on holder, join yarn at neck edge and work the 34 sts for left back. Dec 1 st at each neck edge every row 4 times. Place rem 30 sts on holder to be joined later to front.

FRONT

Work same as back except start neck shaping after 2 rows of yoke, instead of 1" (2.5 cm).

SLEEVES

Make 2.

With size 4 (4, 5, 5) straight needles and A, CO 50, (52, 54, 56) sts. K1, p1 in rib for 2" (5 cm), end with a WS row.

Next row: K, inc 10 sts evenly spaced across row—60 (62, 64, 66) sts. Change to size 7 needles. Cont in St st, inc 1 st each side every 1" (2.5 cm) 15 (17, 19, 21) times—90 (96, 102, 108) sts. Work even until sleeve measures 21 (21½, 22, 22½)" [53 (54.5, 56, 57) cm] from beg. BO loosely.

NECKBAND

With RS facing, join shoulders to back and front using the 3-needle BO method.

With size 4 (4, 5, 5) circular needle, starting at back right shoulder, using A, pick up 12 sts along shaped neck edge of right back, k23 from back holder, pick up 12 sts along shaped neck edge of left back, pick up 14 sts along shaped neck edge of left front, k23 from front holder, pick up 14 sts along shaped neck edge of right front—98 (98, 98, 98) sts. Mark end of round. K1, p1 in rib for 6 rounds. BO loosely in rib.

FINISHING

Fold sleeve in half. Mark center of sleeve and pin to shoulder seam. Pin sleeve in place, then sew in sleeve. Sew underarm seams.

Blocking is not recommended for this stitch pattern.

FRONT AND BACK

6½" [16.5 cm]   10" [25.5 cm]

9 (9½, 10, 10½)" [23 (24, 25.5, 26.5) cm]

15 (15½, 16, 16½)" [38 (39.5, 40.5, 42) cm]

23 (25)" [58.5 (63.5) cm]

SLEEVE

18 (19, 20, 21)" [46 (48, 51, 53) cm]

21 (21½, 22, 22½)" [53 (54.4, 56, 57) cm]

9 (10, 11, 12)" [23 (25.5, 28, 30.5) cm]

YARN

Medium-weight wool 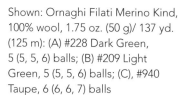 in three colors

Shown: Ornaghi Filati Merino Kind, 100% wool, 1.75 oz. (50 g)/ 137 yd. (125 m): (A) #228 Dark Green, 5 (5, 5, 6) balls; (B) #209 Light Green, 5 (5, 5, 6) balls; (C), #940 Taupe, 6 (6, 6, 7) balls

NEEDLES

Sizes 5 (3.75 mm) and 8 (5 mm) or sizes needed to obtain correct gauge

Size 5 (3.75 mm) double-pointed needles

GAUGE

19 sts = 4" (10 cm) on size 8 needles in St st

Take time to check gauge.

NOTIONS

Six stitch holders

Nine bobbins for holding yarn

SIZES

Small (Medium, Large, X-Large)

Finished chest measurement: 44 (46, 48, 50)" [111.5 (116.5, 122, 127) cm]

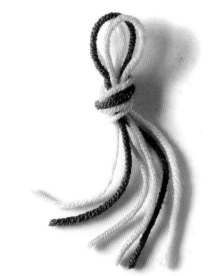

Bold Vertical Stripes

Bold vertical stripes give a long, lean look, which is very flattering for most men. Give the sweater an updated look with a high-contrast color combo like these light and dark greens. To work the frequent color changes without getting your yarn balls tangled, wind the yarn onto bobbins first.

Narrow bands of garter stitch separate wide bands of stockinette stitch worked vertically on the front and back.

For the sleeves, the stripes are worked horizontally.

Notes:

1 Before beginning, wind 4 bobbins with A, 2 with B, and 3 with C. It will be necessary to refill bobbins as you progress.

2 When changing colors, always pick up the new color under the previous color worked to prevent leaving a hole in your work.

BACK

With size 5 straight needles and A, CO 106 (110, 114, 118) sts. K1, p1 in rib for 2½" (6.4 cm), inc 1 st at end of last row, end with a WS row—107 (111, 115, 119) sts. End off A.

Change to size 8 needles and work stripes as foll:

Row 1 (RS): Using yarn wound on bobbins (do not end colors but carry up each row), use a separate bobbin for each color stripe. With C, k15 (17, 19, 21); with A, k5; with B, k19; with A, k5; with C, k19; with A, k5; with B, k19; with A, k5; with C, k15 (17, 19, 21).

Row 2: With C, p15 (17, 19, 21); with A, k5; with B, p19; with A, k5; with C, p19; with A, k5; with B, p19; with A, k5; with C, p15 (17, 19, 21).

Rep Rows 1 and 2 until piece measures 15 (15½, 16, 16½)" [38 (39, 40.5, 42) cm] from beg, end with a WS row.

Shape armholes: Being sure to keep pat as established, BO 5 sts at beg of next 2 rows—97 (101, 105, 109) sts. Work even until armholes measure 9 (9½, 10, 10½)" [23 (24, 25.5, 26.5) cm], end with a WS row.

With RS facing, work across 30 (32, 34, 36) sts and place on holder to be joined to left front shoulder, work across next 37 (37, 37, 37) sts and place on holder to be worked later for back of neckband, work next 30 (32, 34, 36) sts and place on holder to be joined to right front shoulder. End off yarn.

FRONT

Work same as back until armholes measure 6 (6½, 7, 7½)" [15 (16.5, 18, 19) cm], end with a WS row.

Shape neck: Work 34 (36, 38, 40) sts for left front, place next 29 sts on holder for center front neckband, place rem 34 (36, 38, 40) sts on another holder for right front. Keeping pat as established, dec 1 st at neck edge every row 4 times. Work even on rem 30 (32, 34, 36) sts until armhole is same as back to shoulder. Place sts on holder to be joined to back. End off yarn.

Leave 29 center sts on holder, join yarn at neck edge and work the 34 (36, 38, 40) sts for right front. Keeping pat as established, dec 1 st at neck edge every row 4 times. Work even on rem 30 (32, 34, 36) sts until armhole is same as back to shoulder. Place sts on holder to be joined to back. End off yarn.

SLEEVES

Make 2.

STRIPING PATTERN FOR SLEEVES

4 (10 cm) color B

1 (2.5 cm) color A

4 (10 cm) color C

1 (2.5 cm) color A

4 (10 cm) color B

1 (2.5 cm) color A

With size 5 straight needles and A, CO 52 (54, 56, 58) sts. K1, p1 in rib for 2 (2, 2½, 2½)" [5 (5, 6, 6) cm], end with a WS row.

Next row: K, and inc 6 sts evenly spaced across row—58 (60, 62, 64) sts.

Change to size 8 needles. P 1 row.

For X-Large only: K 1 row, p 1 row more.

Follow striping pat; AND AT THE SAME TIME, inc 1 st each side every 1" (2.5 cm) 14 (15, 17, 18) times—86 (90, 96, 100) sts. When incs are completed, cont working until striping pat is completed. BO loosely.

NECKBAND

With RS together, join shoulders with 3-needle BO method.

With RS facing you, using dp needles and starting at back right shoulder, k37 sts from back holder onto 1st needle; with 2nd needle, pick up and k20 (21, 22, 23) along shaped left front, k15 from center front holder; using 3rd needle, k rem 14 sts from center front holder, then pick up and k20 (21, 22, 23) along right front shaping—106 (108, 110, 112) sts: 37 sts on 1st needle, 35 (36, 37, 38) sts on 2nd needle, 34 (35, 36, 37) sts on 3rd needle.

Note: You will now work neckband in rounds. K1, p1 in rib for 1" (2.5 cm). BO loosely in rib.

FINISHING

Fold sleeve in half. Mark center of sleeve and pin to center of shoulder seam. Pin sleeve in place, then sew in sleeve. Sew sleeve and underarm seams.

To block, lay garment on a towel, spritz liberally with water, pat into shape, place another towel on top, and allow to dry.

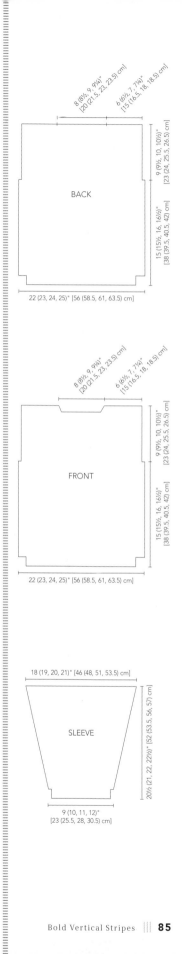

YARN

Medium-weight yarn

Shown: Fixation by Cascade Yarns, 98.3% cotton/1.7% elastic, 1.75 oz. (50 g)/100 yd. (94 m): #9843, 13 (13, 14, 15) skeins

NEEDLES

Sizes 5 (3.75 mm) and 9 (5.5 mm) or sizes needed to obtain correct gauge

Size 5 (3.75 mm) circular needle, 29" (73.5 cm) long

GAUGE

22 sts = 4" (10 cm) on size 9 needles in pat

Take time to check gauge.

NOTIONS

Three stitch holders

SIZES

Small (Medium, Large, X-Large)

Finished chest measurement: 44 (46, 48, 50)" [111.5 (116.5, 122, 127) cm]

Saddle Shoulder Crew

Saddle shoulders often provide a better fit for men. This body-hugging sweater is knit in a rib pattern using cotton yarn that has a small amount of elastic to help it retain its shape. The yarn continually changes color as you knit, creating a free-spirited striping effect.

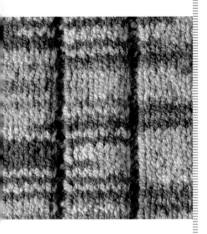

A wide rib pattern makes this sweater very easy to knit.

Saddle shoulders provide a better fit, especially for athletic men.

BACK

With size 5 straight needles, CO 118 (126, 134, 142) sts.

Work border as foll:

Row 1: K2, *p2, k2, rep from * across row.

Row 2: P2, *k2, p2, rep from * across row.

Rep Rows 1 and 2 until border is 2" (5 cm).

Change to size 9 needles and work rib pat as foll:

Row 1 (RS): K6, *p2, k6, rep from * across row.

Row 2: P6, *k2, p6, rep from * across row.

Rep rib pat Rows 1 and 2 until back is 15 (15½, 16, 16½)" [38 (39.5, 40.5, 42) cm] from beg, end with a WS row.

Shape armholes: At beg of next 2 rows, BO 6 (6, 6, 6) sts.

Next row: K2, sl 1, k1, psso, work pat as established to last 4 sts, k2tog, k2.

Next row: P4, work pat until last 4 sts, p4.

Rep last 2 rows 4 times more—96 (104, 112, 120) sts. Work even until armholes measure 7½ (8, 8½, 9)" [19 (20.5, 21.5, 23) cm], end with a WS row.

Saddle shoulder: At beg of next 2 rows, BO 26 (28, 30, 32) sts. Place rem 44 (48, 52, 56) sts on holder to be worked later for neckband.

FRONT

Work same as back until armholes measure 6½ (7, 7½, 8)" [16.5 (18, 19.5, 21) cm], end with a WS row.

Shape neck: Work 30 (32, 34, 36) sts for left front, place center 36 (40, 44, 48) sts on holder for neckband, place rem 30 (32, 34, 36) sts on holder for right front.

Working on left front only, dec 1 st at neck edge every other row 4 times. Work even on rem 26 (28, 30, 32) sts until same as back to shoulder. BO.

Leave center 36 (40, 44, 48) sts on holder, join yarn at neck edge and work the 30 (32, 34, 36) sts for right front. Dec 1 st at neck edge every other row 4 times. Work even until same as back to shoulder. BO rem 26 (28, 30, 32) sts.

SLEEVES

Make 2.

Using size 5 straight needles, CO 62 (70, 70, 78) sts. Work border pat as back for 2" (5 cm).

Change to size 9 needles. Work pat as for back for 2 rows. Inc 1 st each side of next row, then every 6th row 13 (14, 15, 16) times, being sure to keep added sts in pat—90 (100, 102, 112) sts. Work even as est until sleeve is 16½ (17, 17½, 18)" [42 (43, 44.5, 45.5) cm] from beg, end with a WS row.

Shape cap: At beg of next 2 rows, BO 6 (6, 6, 6) sts. Dec 1 st each side same as for back on next row, then every other row 26 (28, 29, 32) times more—24 (30, 30, 34) sts. Work even until cap measures 7½ (8, 8½, 9)" [19 (20.5, 22, 23.5) cm]. At beg of next 2 rows, BO 1 (4, 4, 6) sts. Work pat on rem 22 (22, 22, 22) sts for 4¾ (5, 5½, 6)" [12 (12.5, 14, 15) cm]. BO.

NECKBAND

Pin cap of sleeve and saddle shoulder in place and sew. Sew sleeve and underarm seams.

With RS facing you, using circular size 5 needle, starting at right back of neck, k44 (48, 52, 56) sts from back neck holder, pick up and k22 sts from end of saddle shoulder, pick up and k6 (6, 4, 4) sts along shaped edge of left front, k36 (40, 44, 48) from front neck holder, pick up and k6 (6, 4, 4) sts along shaped edge of right front, pick up and k22 from end of saddle—136 (144, 148, 156) sts. Join and mark end of round.

K2, p2 in rib for 1" (2.5 cm). BO in rib.

FINISHING

Due to the elastic nature of the yarn, blocking is not recommended for this garment. It has lots of stretch. If blocking is desired, lay garment on a towel, spritz with water, pat into shape, and allow to dry.

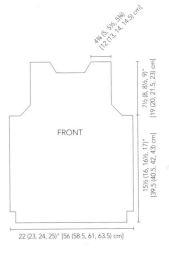

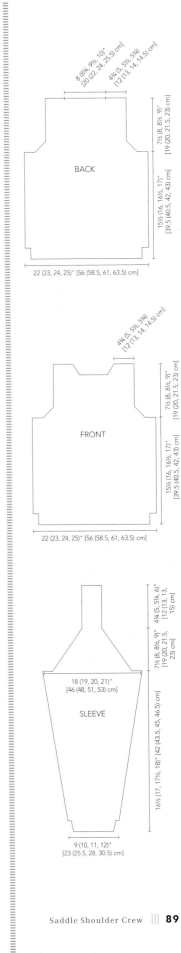

YARN

Medium-weight ribbon yarn (4 MEDIUM)

Shown: Cornucopia by Kollage, 100% corn, 1.19 oz. (34 g)/100 yd. (94 m): (A) Riverview, 12 (12, 13, 14) skeins; (B) Radicchio, 1 (1, 1, 1) skein; (C) Wine, 1 (1, 1, 1) skein; (D) Sapphire, 1 (1, 1, 1) skein

NEEDLES

Sizes 4 (3.5 mm) and 8 (5 mm) or sizes needed to obtain correct gauge

GAUGE

20 sts = 4" (10 cm) on size 8 needles in St st

Take time to check gauge.

NOTIONS

Six buttons, ¾" (1.9 cm) diameter

Six stitch holders

Three bobbins

SIZES

Small (Medium, Large, X-Large)

Finished chest measurement: 44 (46, 48, 50)" [111.5 (116.5, 122, 127) cm]

Argyle Cardigan

The argyle sweater is a true classic and a perennial favorite in men's fashions. This version is updated in bright pastel yarns made entirely from corn fiber . . . yes, corn! At first, I was skeptical about using this ribbon yarn for a man's cardigan, but the results were amazing. The sweater is lightweight and comfortable, perfect for any season, and you can wash and dry it by machine.

The three yarn colors for working the argyle pattern are wound on bobbins. See page 108 for advice on working with yarn bobbins.

Note: Before beginning fronts, wind bobbins with colors B, C, and D.

BACK

With size 4 needles and A, CO 110 (115, 120, 125) sts. K1, p1 in rib for 2½" (6.5 cm). Change to size 8 needles. Work in St st until back is 15 (15½, 16, 16½)" [38 (39.5, 40.5, 42) cm] from beg, end with a WS row.

Shape armholes: At beg of next 2 rows, BO 5 sts. Work even on rem 100 (105, 110, 115) sts until armhole measures 9 (9½, 10, 10½)" [23 (24, 25.5, 26.5) cm], end with a WS row.

Next row: K32 (33, 34, 35), place sts just worked on holder, BO next 36 (39, 42, 45) sts, k rem 32 (33, 34, 35) sts and place on holder.

RIGHT FRONT

With size 4 needles and A, CO 63 (65, 67, 69) sts.

Border pat:

Row 1 (RS): K7, *k1, p1, rep from * across row.

Row 2: *K1, p1, rep from * to last 7 sts, k7.

Rep Rows 1 and 2 for 2½" (6.5 cm), end with a WS row. Change to size 8 needles.

Work main body as foll:

Row 1 (RS): K across row.

Row 2: P to last 7 sts, k7.

Rep last 2 rows 6 (8, 10, 12) times more—8 (10, 12, 14) rows before starting argyle pat.

Foll argyle chart throughout, keeping 7 sts at front edge in garter st and rem sts in St st until same as back to armhole, end with an RS row.

Shape armhole: At beg of next row, BO 5 sts, p across to last 7 sts, k7.

Cont in St st and garter st at front edge; AT THE SAME TIME, beg neck shaping as foll:

Row 1 (RS): K8, sl 1, k1, psso, foll pat to end of row.

Row 2: P to last 7 sts, k7.

Row 3: K across row.

Row 4: Rep Row 2.

Rep Rows 1–4 once more.

Rep Rows 1 and 2 until 39 (40, 41, 42) sts rem. Work even until piece measures same as back to shoulder, end with an RS row.

Next row: P32 (33, 34, 35) sts and place on holder. Cont in garter st on rem 7 sts for 3½ (3¾, 4, 4¼)" [9 (9.5, 10, 11) cm] measured when slightly stretched. Place 7 sts on holder.

▌LEFT FRONT

Note: On buttonhole side, mark right front as guide for even placement of 6 buttonholes, having the first buttonhole ½" (1.25 cm) from the bottom and the last buttonhole at the beginning of the V-neck shaping.

Make 6 buttonholes on the 7 front garter sts as foll:

RS row: K3, yo, k2tog, k2.

WS row: K7.

With size 4 needles and A, CO 63 (65, 67, 69) sts.

Border pat:

Row 1 (RS): *P1, k1, rep from * to last 7 sts, k7.

Row 2: K7, *p1, k1, rep from * across row.

Rep Rows 1 and for 2½" (6.5 cm), end with a WS row. Change to size 8 needles and work main body as foll:

Row 1 (RS): K across row.

Row 2: P to last 7 sts, k7.

Rep last 2 rows 6 (8, 10, 12) times more—8 (10, 12, 14) rows before starting Argyle pat.

Foll Argyle chart throughout, keeping 7 sts at front edge in garter st and rem sts in St st, until same as back to armhole, end with a WS row.

Shape armhole: At beg of next row, BO 5 sts, k across to last 7 sts, k7.

Cont in St st and garter st at front edge; AT THE SAME TIME, beg neck shaping as foll:

Row 1 (RS): Follow pat to last 9 sts, k2tog, k7.

Row 2: K7, p across row.

Row 3: K across row.

Row 4: Rep Row 2.

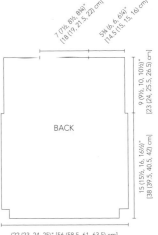

BACK

7 (7½, 8½, 8¾)"
[18 (19, 21.5, 22) cm]

5¾ (6, 6, 6¼)"
[14.5 (15, 15, 16) cm]

9 (9½, 10, 10½)"
[23 (24, 25.5, 26.5) cm]

15 (15½, 16, 16½)"
[38 (39.5, 40.5, 42) cm]

(22 (23, 24, 25)" [56 (58.5, 61, 63.5) cm]

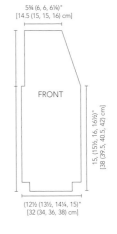

FRONT

5¾ (6, 6, 6¼)"
[14.5 (15, 15, 16) cm]

15 (15½, 16, 16½)"
[38 (39.5, 40.5, 42) cm]

(12½ (13½, 14¼, 15)"
[32 (34, 36, 38) cm]

SLEEVE

18 (19, 20, 21)" [46 (48, 51, 53) cm

21 (21½, 22, 22½)"
[53 (54.5, 56, 57) cm]

10¾ (11, 11½, 12)"
[27 (28, 29, 30.5) cm]

Rep Rows 1–4 once more.

Rep Rows 1 and 2 until 39 (40, 41, 42) sts rem. Work even until same as back to shoulder, end with a WS row.

Next row: K32 (33, 34, 35) sts and place on holder. Cont in garter st on rem 7 sts for 3½ (3¾, 4, 4¼)" [9 (9.5, 10, 11) cm] measured when slightly stretched. Place 7 sts on holder.

SLEEVES

Make 2.

With size 4 needles and A, CO 56 (58, 60, 62) sts. K1, p1 in rib for 2½" (6.5 cm).

Next row: P across, inc 4 sts evenly spaced across row—60 (62, 64, 66) sts.

Change to size 8 needles. Work in St st, inc 1 st each side every 1" (2.5 cm) 15 (16, 17, 18) times. Work even on 90 (94, 98, 102) sts until sleeve measures 21 (21½, 22, 22½)" [53.5 (54.5, 56, 57) cm] from beg. BO loosely.

FINISHING

Holding RS together, join fronts to back using three-needle BO method.

Join short end of both neck tabs using three-needle BO method.

Pin seam to center back of neck; sew neckband in place.

Fold sleeve in half. Mark center of sleeve and pin to shoulder seam. Pin sleeve in place, then sew in sleeve. Sew side and underarm seams. Sew on buttons opposite buttonholes.

If blocking is desired, lay out on a towel, spritz with water, gently pat into shape, and allow to dry.

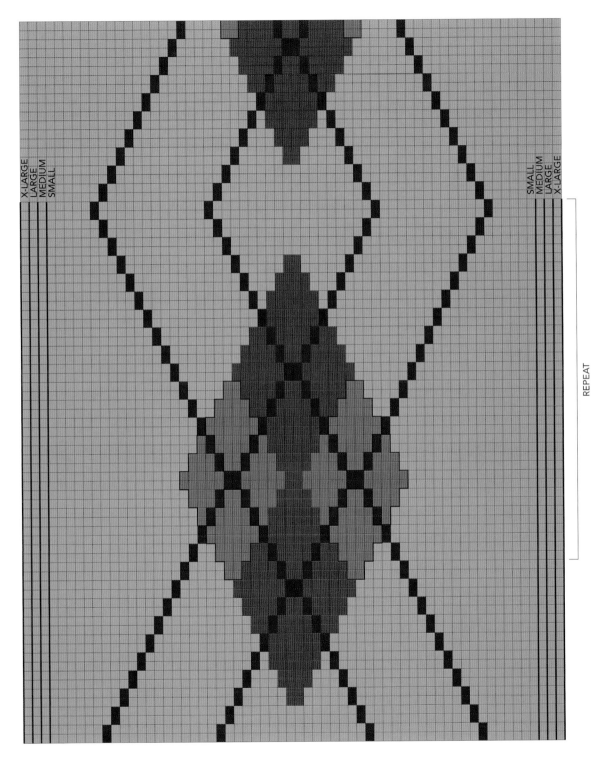

■ Main Color A   SMALL: (56 + 7 Border)

■ Color B   MEDIUM: (58 + 7 Border)

■ Color C   LARGE: (60 + 7 Border)

■ Color D   X-LARGE: (62 + 7 Border)

Ski Hat and Scarf

Create a little excitement on the slopes. This ski hat and scarf feature a two-color slip-stitch pattern that looks tricky but really isn't. They're made with bulky-weight yarn, so the knitting goes quickly. Earflaps have I-cord ties and there's an extra cord at the top just for fun.

YARN

Bulky acrylic/wool **[5 BULKY]**

Shown: Encore Chunky by Plymouth, 75% acrylic/25% wool, 3.5 oz. (100 g)/143 yd. (132 m): (A) #133 Blue, 2 skeins; (B) #1382 Bright Yellow, 2 skeins

NEEDLES

Sizes 6 (4 mm) and 9 (5.5 mm) for hat

Size 6 (4 mm) double-pointed needles for I-cord

Size 10½ (6.5 mm) for scarf

or sizes needed to obtain correct gauge

GAUGE

13 sts = 4" (10 cm) on size 9 needles in Sl-st pat

Take time to check gauge.

NOTIONS

Tapestry needle

SIZE

Hat: 22" (56 cm) head circumference

Scarf: 9" x 60" (23 x 152.5 cm)

This stitch pattern looks intricate but the design is easily created with slip stiches.

Notes:

1 The yarn amounts listed make both the scarf and the hat. To make just the scarf, you need only 1 skein of A and 1 skein of B. To make just the hat, you need only 1 skein of A and 1 skein of B.

2 Do not break yarn after each color change; instead, carry loosely up sides, twisting at the end of every other row.

HAT

With size 6 needles and A, CO 73 sts. Work border pat as foll:

Rows 1 and 2: With A, k across row.

Rows 3 and 4: With B, k across row.

Rows 5 and 6: With A, k across row.

Rows 7 and 8: With B, k across row.

Rows 9 and 10: With A, k across row.

Change to size 9 needles. Work Sl-st pat for 20 rows as foll:

Row 1 (WS): With B, p across row.

Row 2: With A, k1, *yarn back (yb), sl 1, yarn front (yf), sl 1, yb, sl 1, k1, rep from * across row.

Row 3: With A, p1, *yb, sl 3, wrap yarn around needle, p1, rep from * across row.

Row 4: With B, k across row, dropping extra wraps to make long loose strands in front of work.

Row 5: With B, p across row.

Row 6: With A, k1, *yb, sl 1, insert needle from the front under the loose strand and k the loose strand and the next st as one, yb, sl 1, k1, rep from * across row.

Row 7: With A, k1, *yf, sl 1, p1, yf, sl 1, k1, rep from * across row.

Row 8: With B, k across row.

Row 9: With B, p across row.

Row 10: With A, k1, *yf, sl 1, yb, k1, rep from * across row.

Rows 11–20: Rep Rows 1–10, reversing colors.

Row 21: Rep Row 1.

Rows 22–31: Cont using size 9 needles, rep 10 border rows. End off B.

Shape top of hat, working with A, as foll:

Row 1 (RS): K1, k2tog, *k7, k2tog, rep from * 6 times more, end k5, k2tog— 64 sts.

Row 2: P8, place marker, p16, place marker, p16, place marker, p16, place marker, p8.

Row 3: Slipping markers as you work, k to within 2 sts of first marker, sl 1, k1, psso, sl marker, k2tog, rep from * 3 times more, end k6 (8 dec made)—56 sts.

Row 4: P across row.

Rep last 2 rows 5 times more—16 sts. Do not BO. Leave a 24" (61 cm) length of yarn. Draw through rem sts. Pull up tightly and knot. Use yarn to sew back seam.

EARFLAPS

Right: With RS facing, using size 6 needles and A, starting 1½" (4 cm) from back seam, pick up 19 sts along CO edge.

Rows 1–7: K across row.

Row 8: K1, k2tog, k to last 3 sts, k2tog, k1.

Row 9: K across row.

Rep Rows 8 and 9 until 5 sts rem.

Knit 1 more row, dec 1 st at end of row. Join B and using both colors together, work an I-cord for 7" (18 cm) as foll:

I-cord: Using dp needles, k4. Switch needles in your hands, so the needle with the sts is in your left hand again. Slide the sts to the other end of the needle and pulling the yarn across the back of the sts, knit the row again. Cont in this manner, sliding and knitting until the cord is the desired length. Give the cord a tug to make the little carry across the back disappear (there shouldn't be much of a carry since you are only knitting on 4 sts).

Leave edges for fringe, then pull through 8 more strands of yarn at end for more fringe.

Left: Work same as right earflap starting 1½" (4 cm) from back seam.

Top of hat I-cord: Make another 2-color, 7" (18 cm) I-cord and sew to top of hat.

SCARF

Make 2 pieces alike.

With size 10½" (6.5 mm) needles and B, CO 29 sts. Knit 2 rows.

Work 21 rows of Sl-st pat as for hat.

Start rib pat as foll:

Row 1: K1, *p1, k1, rep from * across row.

Row 2: P1, *k1, p1, rep from * across row.

Rep last 2 rows until piece measures 30" (76 cm); do not BO.

Holding RS of 2 pieces together, join 2 A edges with three-needle BO method.

Evenly spaced decreases mold the top of the hat to fit the head.

YARN

Medium-weight yarn

Shown: Dolce by Cascade Yarns, 55% superfine alpaca/23% wool/22% silk, 1.75 oz. (50 g)/109 yd. (100 m): (A) # 933 natural, 4 skeins; (B) #912 light brown, 3 skeins; (C) #924 dark brown, 1 skein

NEEDLES

Sizes 6 (4 mm) and 8 (11 mm) or sizes needed to obtain correct gauge

GAUGE

20 sts = 4" (10 cm) in St st

Take time to check gauge.

NOTIONS

Tapestry needle

SIZES

Hat: 22" (56 cm) head circumference

Scarf: 7" x 60" (18 x 152.5 cm)

Roll-Brim Hat and Scarf

Style and warmth go hand-in-hand with this hat and scarf duo. The yarn is a luxurious alpaca, wool, and silk blend. The double-rolled brim on the hat will take on any Arctic chill and win. The textured design is another winner, created with an exceptionally easy slip-stitch technique.

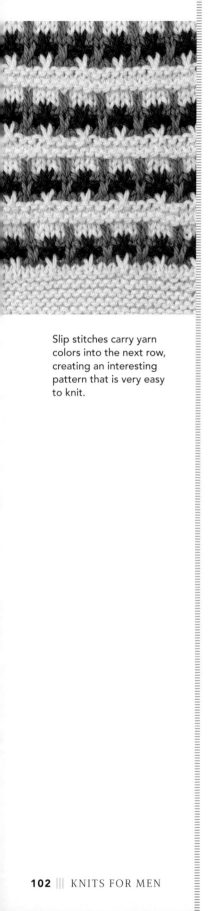

Slip stitches carry yarn colors into the next row, creating an interesting pattern that is very easy to knit.

Notes:

1 The yarn amounts listed make both the scarf and the hat. To make just the scarf, you need only 2 skeins of A, 2 skeins of B, and 1 skein of C. To make just the hat, you need only 2 skeins of A, 1 skein of B, and 1 skein of C.

2 Do not break yarn at end of every stripe; instead, carry yarn up sides, twisting at the end of every other row.

SCARF

Make 2 pieces alike.

With size 8 needles and A, CO 35 sts. Knit 6 rows.

Begin pat as foll:

Rows 1–4: With A, k across row.

Row 5: With B, k3, *sl 1, k3, rep from * across row.

Row 6: With B, p3, *sl 1, p3, rep from * across row.

Row 7: With C, k1, *sl 1, k3, rep from * to last 2 sts, end sl 1, k1.

Row 8: With C, k1, *yarn front (yf), sl 1, yarn back (yb), k3, rep from * to last 2 sts, end yf, sl 1, yb, k1.

Rows 9 and 10: With B, rep Rows 5 and 6.

Row 11: With A, rep Row 7.

Row 12: With A, p1, *sl 1, p3, rep from * to last 2 sts, end sl 1, p1.

Rep pat Rows 1–12, 17 times more, then rep Rows 1 and 2 once. Place all sts on holder to be joined at center.

FINISHING

Holding RS together, using the three-needle BO method, join both pieces.

To block, fold scarf in half, lay on a towel, spritz with water, pat into shape, and allow to dry.

HAT

With size 6 needles and A, CO 106 sts. K1, p1 in rib for 6" (15 cm), end with a WS row and inc 1 st at end of last row—107 sts.

Change to size 8 needles and work pat as foll:

Rows 1–4: K across row.

Row 5 (RS): With B, k3, *sl 1, k3, rep from * across row.

Row 6: With B, p3, *sl 1, p3, rep from * across row.

Row 7: With C, k1, *sl 1, k3, rep from * to last 2 sts, end sl 1, k1.

Row 8: With C, k1, *yf, sl 1, yb, k3, rep from * to last 2 sts, end yf, sl 1, yb, k1.

Rows 9 and 10: With B, rep Rows 5 and 6.

Row 11: With A, rep Row 7.

Row 12: With A, p1, *sl 1, p3, rep from * to last 2 sts, end sl 1, p1.

Rep pat Rows 1–12 once more.

Rep pat Rows 1–4 once, dec 3 sts evenly spaced across last row—104 sts.

Shape top of hat:

Row 1 (RS): *K6, k2tog, rep from * across row.

Row 2: P across row.

Row 3: *K5, k2tog, rep from * across row.

Row 4: P across row.

Row 5: *K4, k2tog, rep from * across row.

Row 6: P across row.

Cont dec 13 sts each knit row, always having 1 st less between dec until 13 sts rem; do not BO. Cut yarn, leaving a 24" (61 cm) length of yarn.

FINISHING

Draw yarn through rem sts. Pull up tightly and knot. Using same yarn, sew back seam, weaving the ribbed end. This ribbed end is folded twice to form the rolled brim.

YARN

Medium-weight alpaca **[4 MEDIUM]**

Shown: Inca Alpaca by Classic Elite, 100% alpaca, 1.75 oz. (50 g)/109 yd. (100 m): (A) #1146 Teal, 4 skeins; (B) #1110 Light Blue, 1 skein; (C) #1159 Navy, 1 skein

NEEDLES

Sizes 5 (3.75 mm), 7 (4.5 mm), and 8 (5 mm) or sizes needed to obtain correct gauge

Size 5 (3.75 mm) double-pointed needles

GAUGE

20 sts = 4" (10 cm) on size 7 needles in Sl-st pat

18 sts = 4" (10 cm) on size 8 needles in Sl-st pat

Take time to check gauge.

NOTIONS

Stitch holder

Pair of Fiber Trends Suede slipper bottoms

SIZES

Small (Medium, Large)

Finished foot length: 10 (10½, 11)" [25.5 (26.5, 28) cm]

Après-Ski Slipper Sox

After a day of skiing or for just lounging around the house, these knitted boots with nonslip bottoms will keep his feet warm and toasty.

The socks feature a two-color slip-stitch design that looks intricate but is really easy to achieve.

Notes:

1 Straight needles are used until the heel is turned, then the foot is completed on dp needles.

2 Do not break yarn after each color change; instead carry yarn loosely up sides.

3 When sewing on heel and toe pads, place a rolled-up magazine in the socks to make sewing easier.

SLIPPER SOX

Make 2.

With size 5 straight needles and A, CO 70 (70, 70) sts. K2, p2 in rib for 6" (15 cm), inc 1 st at end of last row, end with a WS row—71 (71, 71, 71) sts.

Change to size 7 (7, 8) needles, begin pat as foll:

Rows 1–4: With A, k across row.

Row 5: With B, k3, *sl 1, k3, rep from * across row.

Row 6: With B, p3, *sl 1, p3, rep from * across row.

Row 7: With C, k1, *sl 1, k3, rep from * to last 2 sts, end sl 1, k1.

Row 8: With C, k1, * yarn front (yf), sl 1, yarn back (yb), k3, rep from * to last 2 sts, end yf, sl 1, yb, k1.

Rows 9 and 10: With B, rep Rows 5 and 6.

Row 11: With A, rep Row 7.

Row12: With A, p1, *sl 1, p3, rep from * to last 2 sts, end sl 1, p1.

Rep pat Rows 1–12, 3 times more (48 pat rows in all).

Change to size 5 (5, 7) needles. Work 48 more pat rows. End off B and C; complete sock with A. Cont with size 5 needles for all sizes.

Next row: K5, *k2tog, k4, rep from * across row—60 sts. End off yarn.

Work heel:

Sl first 15 sts onto a dp needle (half heel sts), sl next 30 sts on holder to be worked later for instep, sl last 15 sts to a dp needle (other half of heel).

Work the 30 heel sts as follows:

Row 1: Sl 1, k across row.

Row 2: *Sl 1, p1, rep from * across row.

Rep Rows 1 and 2 until heel measures 2 (2¼, 2½)" [5 (5.5, 6.4) cm].

Turn heel:

K19, turn, sl 1, p10, turn.

Sl 1, k9, k2tog, k1, turn.

Sl 1, p10, p2tog, p1, turn.

Sl 1, k11, k2tog, k1, turn.

Sl 1, p12, p2tog, p1, turn.

Sl 1, k13, k2tog, k1, turn.

Sl 1, p14, p2tog, p1, turn.

Sl 1, k15, k2tog, k1, turn.

Sl 1, p16, p2tog, p1, turn.

Sl 1, k17, k2tog, k1, turn.

P20.

Work foot:

With RS facing and using size 5 dp needles, knit 20 heel sts, pick up 12 (13, 14) sts along one side of heel (this is 1st needle); with 2nd needle, k30 sts from holder for instep; with 3rd needle, pick up 12 (13, 14) sts along other side of heel, k10 sts from 1st needle onto 3rd needle. Join, begin working in rounds. You will now have sts divided onto 3 dp needles: 1st needle will have 22 (23, 24) sts, 2nd needle will have 30 sts, 3rd needle will have 22 (23, 24) sts. Mark center of heel as beg of round.

Round 1: On 1st needle, k20 (21, 22), k2tog; on 2nd needle, k30; on 3rd needle, k2tog, k20 (21, 22).

Rep Round 1, 6 (7, 8) times more. You will now have 15 sts on 1st needle, 30 sts on 2nd needle, 15 sts on 3rd needle—60 sts.

Cont working in rounds, knitting every row until foot measures 7 (7½, 8)" [18 (19, 20.5) cm], or 3" (7.5 cm) less than desired finished length from bottom of heel.

Shape toe:

Round 1: With 1st needle, k to last 3 sts, k2tog, k1; with 2nd needle, k1, sl 1, k1, psso, k to last 3 sts, k2tog, k1; with 3rd needle, k1, sl 1, k1, psso, k to end.

Round 2: K all sts.

Rep Rounds 1 and 2 until 16 sts rem. You will have 4 sts on 1st needle, 8 sts on 2nd needle, 4 sts on 3rd needle. Knit the 4 sts from 1st needle onto 3rd needle. You now have 2 needles with 8 sts on each. Graft these sts together to form toe closing. See page 110.

FINISHING

Sew back seam. Pin heel and toe patches in place and sew using A.

Blocking is not recommended for this pattern stitch.

Suede sole patches are made by Fiber Trends. Look for them at your favorite yarn shop. Alternatively, cut your own from suede scraps and punch holes around the edges for hand-sewing to the socks.

IIII Knitting Basics

Here are some of the techniques you will encounter as you knit the projects.

PAIRED DECREASES

Decreases are often paired with one at each side of the piece at arm edges, necklines, sock toes, etc. For the best appearance, the paired stitches should slant in opposite directions, away from the edge of the piece. The decrease is usually made on the second stitch from the edge. The following instructions are for paired decreases worked in stockinette, and both decreases are made from the right side.

Left slant: K1, sl 1, k1, psso.

Knit the first stitch, slip the second stitch, knit the third stitch, then pass the slipped stitch over the last stitch.

Right slant: K2tog.

Knit to within 3 stitches of the end. Insert the needle into the front loops of the next two stitches, first through the second stitch and then through the first. Knit the stitches together.

YARN BOBBINS

When you will be changing colors frequently, wind yarn onto bobbins. When changing colors, always pick up the new color *under* the previous color worked to prevent leaving a hole in your work.

I-CORD

Narrow knitted tubes, called I-cords, are often used for ties on hats or as knitted embellishments. You will need double-pointed needles to make I-cords.

1 Cast on the number of stitches needed (usually 2 to 4).

2 Knit the stitches, but do not turn.

3 Slide the stitches to the opposite end of the needle.

4 Bring the yarn across the back of the stitches and pull tight. Knit the next row.

5 Repeat steps 3 and 4 until the cord is the desired length.

6 Break the yarn, leaving a 6" (15 cm) tail. Use a tapestry needle to draw the tail through the remaining stitches.

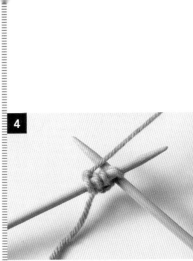

THREE-NEEDLE BIND-OFF

Use this method to join two sets of live stitches in a seam, such as for shoulder seams.

1 Place the two pieces right sides together, aligning the needles, and hold the needles in your left hand. Insert a third needle, knitwise, through the first stitch on both needles, first through the front needle and then through the back one. Using the yarn tail at the end of either row, wrap the yarn over and complete the stitch.

2 Complete a second stitch as in step 1. Now slip the first stitch over the second stitch, to bind it off. Continue knitting and binding off in this manner to the end of the seam.

▌ GRAFTING

Grafting, also called kitchener stitch, weaves together two rows of "live" stitches (not bound off), resulting in an invisible joining.

1 Cut the working yarn, leaving a tail about 18" (46 cm) long. Leave the stitches on the needles; there should be the same number of stitches on each. Hold the needles side by side in your left hand, with the right side facing up. Slide the stitches toward the needle tips.

2 The working yarn will be coming from the first stitch on the back needle. To help explain the steps, I have used a contrasting yarn as the working yarn. Thread the yarn tail onto a yarn needle. Draw the yarn through the first stitch on the front needle as if to purl, and leave the stitch on the needle.

3 Keeping the yarn under the needles, draw the yarn through the first stitch on the back needle as if to knit, and leave the stitch on the needle.

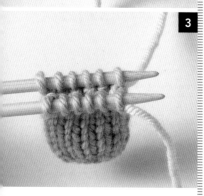

4 Draw the yarn through the first stitch on the front needle as if to knit, and slip the stitch off the needle.

5 Draw the yarn through the next stitch on the front needle as if to purl, and leave the stitch on the needle.

6 Draw the yarn through the first stitch on the back needle as if to purl, and slip the stitch off the needle.

7 Draw the yarn through the next stitch on the back needle as if to knit, and leave the stitch on the needle.

8 Repeat steps 4 through 7 until all the stitches have been worked off the needles.

9 If necessary, use the tip of the yarn needle to adjust the tension of the grafting stitches until the join is invisible. With practice, your grafting will need very little adjustment.

10 Draw the yarn to the wrong side and weave in the tail end.

|||| Dedication

For my children and grandchildren, who constantly fill my life with joy.

|||| Acknowledgments

Many thanks to the following yarn companies for the generous donations of their yarns for the projects in the book: Aurora Yarns, Aussie Wool, Berroco, Brown Sheep Company, Cascade Yarns, Classic Elite, Debbie Bliss, Knitting Fever, Kollage Yarns, Lion Brand Yarn, Louet, Moda Dea Yarns, Ornaghi Filati, Patons, Plymouth Yarn, Seaport Yarn, South West Trading Company, and Tahki Stacy Charles.

Thank you Linda Neubauer, my editor, who is always a pleasure to work with.

I would also like to thank Paula Alexander, Jeannine Buehler, Catherine Brunow, Frances Feery, Lillian Kristiansen, and Marie Stewart for helping me knit some of the items featured in the book.

⫴ Abbreviations

beg	begin	rev St stitch	reverse Stockinette stitch
bet	between	rib	ribbing
BO	bind off	rnd(s)	rounds
CC	contrasting color	RS	right side
cm	centimeters	sk	skip
cn	cable needle	sl	slip
CO	cast on	sl st	slip stitch
cont	continue	ssk	slip, slip, knit decrease
dec	decrease	st(s)	stitch(es)
dpn	double-pointed needle(s)	St st	Stockinette stitch
g	grams	tbl	through back loop
inc	increase	WS	wrong side
k	knit	wyb	with yarn in back
k1f&b	knit into front and back loop of same stitch	wyf	with yarn in front
k2tog	knit two stitches together	yo	yarn over needle
kwise	knitwise	*	repeat from *
m(s)	markers(s)	[]	repeat instructions in brackets as directed
MC	main color	()	number of stitches that should be on the needle or across a row
rem	remaining or remain		
mm	millimeters		
M1	make one stitch (increase)		
p	purl		
p1f&b	pearl into front and back loop of same stitch		
p2tog	pearl two stitches together		
pat	pattern		
pwise	purlwise		
rep	repeat		